Angels From Hell

A Community Approach to Preventing Crime and
Healing Criminals

Byron Elsey

ISBN: 1-4392-4934-2
ISBN-13: 9781439249345

Visit www.booksurge.com to order additional copies.

Dedication

Dedicated to the criminals and their families
whom I have had the privilege of knowing.

Illustrator-Ruth McKay

Table of contents

Introduction:

Angels From Hell: A Community Approach to Preventing Crime and Healing Criminals.

Who are these Angels from hell? These are people who have gone through hell and found a better life. These are criminals and their families. This book is chock full of things I learned as a chaplain for criminals and their families.

There may be nothing new under the sun, but we are living in a new day that needs a new approach to reducing crime. Crime is on the increase in many communities. Our old justice system is not working. A new approach to fighting crime is needed.

The mark of a good community is fair and just dealings among its people. We all want to feel safe in our homes and on our streets. Murder, violence, home invasions, sexual assaults, domestic violence, car theft, break and entries, drug and gang activities, and white-collar crime continue to destroy the lives of many.

The old methods we still use today to reduce crime are not working. The number of re-offences is very high. Prisons are costing more and more. Fear of crime cripples many people's lives. They are afraid to go out at night or even to walk in certain areas of the city in daytime. It is time to do something about the situation we face.

Chapter 1
NO TEARS ALLOWED IN HELL

Our society has an insatiable curiosity about crime. What happened? Where did it happen? When did it happen? This book is concerned with the why of crime. Why did it happen? If we answer this question, we will do a better job of preventing crime.

I have a unique perspective because of my close relationship with over 300 prisoners and ex-prisoners. Being a chaplain counselor, people have shared with me their experiences in a more honest way than with anyone else. They know what they share with me is kept confidential, which means I will not identify anyone with the information they share. I have worked in three correctional institutions as a chaplain, then for many years worked as a community chaplain, counseling criminals and their families. In the community, I was employed by a non-profit board and therefore have a neutral and objective view of the correctional system. Much of the material in this book was used in my individual and group counseling sessions. My experience with criminals has given me the opportunity of getting to know what makes them tick. I know criminals as good friends and members of my family. They are human beings, not unlike other human beings. My approach is Christian, and the ideas expressed

1

in this book are in line with Biblical principles as I understand them.

Many victims and their families are scarred for life by some criminal behavior. When a criminal changes his/her ways, we all benefit. When a criminal's family becomes healthy, everyone benefits. The crininal's children are much less likely to become criminals, as happens in many cases now. It is essential to help criminals and their families if we are going to reduce crime.

There are many reasons as to why criminals commit crime. Criminals are individuals, and their reasons for committing crimes are different. For some it is peer pressure. Their friends are doing crime, so they join them. A young friend of mine was picked up the other day by his friend who had just stolen a car. Both were charged and are in prison. Sometimes a person steals because they need money for drugs or something else. Many come from the homes of the poor and don't have the educational or other opportunities many others have. Often their environment doesn't give them much cause to have hope for a better day.

The criminal may be any family member, a mother, father, son, daughter, brother, sister, etc. Sooner or later, most families will have a member who becomes involved with the justice system either as a criminal or a victim. Most aboriginal males have done time in prison.

Criminals do not live in isolation when released. The most important people in a person's life are their family and friends. Those who succeed in life after prison do so largely because of family and friends. Unfortunately, prison policy isolates people from those who could be most helpful in their successful reintegration into the community.

Most of us have an incomplete understanding of what criminals are like. Sometimes they give us good reason to criticize them. Their behavior is not appropriate. So Jack is put in prison to punish him. This is your fairly simple redneck legalistic attitude: "You broke the law, and we will see you pay. We will get even with you." Such a negative approach doesn't work very well. It just seems to produce negative results. You can't fight evil with evil.

There is another way of looking at Jack. It is not so simple. Jack is just like the rest of us. He is a person. Like us, he gets angry, he experiences fear, suffers pain, sadness, guilt, and healing. Here, Jack is part of a family, the family of man, created in the image of God. His crime affects the entire family. It doesn't begin with breaking the law but with relationships. Here, breaking the law might not be a sin. Mary stole a bottle of milk to feed her starving children. She broke the law, which was wrong and she should be punished. But morally Mary was right. Mary is morally responsible to take care of the needs of her children. We need to

3

look at the root causes. Breaking the law may not be sin. My wife speeds to visit a dying person. Is she guilty or not?

Criminals are not all the same. They are as different as any group of non- criminals We tend to put people in a box and this is wrong. People in any group are very different. They look different, think and act different. They are unique. Though most criminals have been in prison, they have reacted in different ways and to different degrees to their prison experience because of their differences. So let's not label people and put them all in the same box.

There are no tears allowed in prison. Most criminals are scarred by their experience in prison to a greater or lesser degree. Some have physical scars. Most have emotional scars. They feel guilty, unloved, and betrayed. They have little dignity and self-respect. For most, the experience has been traumatic and is now part of the individual's lifetime memory. They have been rejected and find themselves grieving alone. They have also learned not to trust others.

Do criminals change? The answer to this question is a resounding, "yes."

The following true account of Ron is not unusual. It has happened over and over again. Ron is a man who spent from the age of sixteen to thirty-seven in a number of correctional institutions across Canada. Some people deserve better than what life hands them. In Ron's case, his mother died while he was very young. His formal schooling was finished in grade nine. At sixteen, he was placed in a juvenile correctional center for a minor crime in which he was charged as an accomplice. To his death, he denied any involvement in that crime. His only crime was being in the wrong place even though he lived only a few doors down the street from the crime scene. For Ron the door to the youth facility proved to be the door to a new family that introduced him to the world of crime. Things went from bad to worse. For the next twenty years, Ron committed a variety of crimes. In the end, he changed, thanks to the friendships of a number of straight people. He was paroled in his forties, got a good job, a wife, and lived as a productive law abiding citizen for the next twenty-five years. Unfortunately, during those years, he could not get rid of the tag "criminal."

Change is part of life for all of us. Who is the same person at forty-eight years of age as they were at eighteen? Much has happened during those thirty years to change a person. Change and death are two things we can all be sure of. Most people look at the criminal by himself or herself rather than as a member of some family. Every criminal is some mother's son or daughter. Jack committed a crime. We tend to look at Jack through the lens of his crime the rest of his life. We scapegoat those who go to prison. They are treated as less than human. There is a tendency in all of us to blame others. It makes us feel better about ourselves. We are the good guys. They are the bad guys. When we label people instead of understanding them, we are destroying them. We are making matters worse. When we react to violence with more violence, we are just creating more violence. Like it or not, we are all part of the human family by creation and we all do badly. We are not unlike those who go to prison. We are part of the same family—the human family.

We don't ask, "Why did he/she do it?" because we're afraid we may find we are partly responsible for the real reason. Could it be the root cause of this person's involvement with crime is social injustice? What about things like affordable housing, adequate benefits, good health care, opportunities for employment, appropriate educational opportunities? The other day I learned two of my criminal friends had little education. Believe it or not, one of them had no school education at all. The other one had a grade two education. Something is wrong here. Where your basic human rights are not met, there is little hope of a better life and crime rises. These things are seen as injustices by those in need of them. Is our pride, greed, and selfishness part of the reason for some of the crime in our midst?

The environment in which a person lives has a lot to do with whether he commits a crime and goes to prison or not. The fact a person feels rejected and therefore has a poor self-image and little dignity and respect has a lot to do with it. Often basic values like honesty and concern for others have not been implanted in the heart and mind through teaching and example. A person may have little conscience as a result. And then there are their peers, often older, whose way of life is learned. It is not too hard to see why many get involved in a life of crime.

This book deals with many of the problems criminals face and how to deal with them. Their problems are not unlike the problems many of the rest of us face. The causes of crime such as labeling, poor parenting skills, relationship problems, addictions, and violence are dealt with in this book. After criminals have been released from prison, the chapter on taking responsibility and finding a job will be helpful. The chapters on self-esteem, labeling, building relationships, and mentoring will be helpful to those seeking to help criminals. The chapter on how a relationship with God helps is a must-read for everyone. This book is not intended to be a substitute for good individual or group counseling, but it certainly can supplement other help a person may receive.

Chapter 2
CHANGING LABELS

"Labeling" in this book is the name given to a person to describe them to other people in a negative way. It may be used for people who have a handicap: either physical, mental, or some other perceived problem. Even though the term is destructive to a person's self-esteem, it is accepted by them and a tag they will wear the rest of their lives. Society often uses tags such as mental, learning disabled, dumb, lazy, criminal, and difficult.

Labeling often begins at birth. The baby cries a lot, is upset, and is too active. Such a baby is described as a difficult baby. We label a person when they give us good reason to criticize their behavior, particularly if they are weak and vulnerable. A child whose behavior is unacceptable gets labeled. A person who commits a crime gets labeled.

Labeling begins because people are different. The powerful and rich put labels on the poor and weak. It makes the powerful more righteous. It's not their problem, and they are not to blame for it. Just look at those who are in prison. You will likely find people who have been continually labeled and excluded, the aboriginal, the underachiever, and the young. Disadvantaged people will suffer most from labeling. The rich as well as their children will suffer less because of their resources.

At first, labeling was used for a positive purpose, as an administrative tool, to help children who learned in a different way. All humans learn throughout their lives, but they learn in different ways.

The sad little boy has been labeled. He sees himself as different. Other kids shun him. No one wants to be his friend. When the team leader chooses who he wants on his team, this boy is always the last one chosen. The teacher treats him different than the other kids. He goes home alone every day. He gives up trying at school, as he can't keep up with the others.

Labeled students very often become their label. It makes it very hard for them to feel good about themselves and not produce our negative expectations. They are seen as the negative label says they are. This is very limiting. What about their abilities, their strengths, and the things they are learning? Where is the justice here? Kids who are lucky enough to be able to write, read, and do arithmatic according to the school standards are seen as normal human beings. But often the students who fall short in reading, writing, and arithmetic lose their right to be normal human beings. They become those who can't. We all know the results of thinking like this. The snowballing affect will follow them the rest of their days. They can't get an education or a job. We need to come up with a more positive way of dealing with this problem if we are going to reduce the devastating results of labeling people.

Seventy-five years ago things were very different. Family, friends, and neighbors were both willing and able to cope with the anti-social problems of most people in the community. In recent years, people have found themselves isolated even from the neighbor next door. Problems are no longer our problem, so "call the cops" rather than get involved by taking some responsibility. Today an unknown person becomes involved with an unknown police officer who investigates the unknown neighbor's complaint. The person is apt to end up with the label "criminal" and is going to feel he has been rejected by the square world. He will then seek security among other criminals who will accept him as he is. Society relies on means of correction that reinforce a criminal's negative self-concept. We segregate him for months or years, and he concludes we have rejected him. We are very good at killing a person's hope for the future. We justify ourselves by saying he first rejected us and our values.

Long-ago Jesus showed us the way to solve the problem. He did what we find it so hard to do. He accepted people as he found them, and having accepted them, changed them. He rejected their evil deeds but accepted them as people. He said, "Neither do I condemn you, go and sin no more." We hate sin, too, but work out our hostility on the criminal. We will never convert the criminal to our side if we hate and isolate him. To change the criminal we must get close enough to impress him with our values. Jesus did this with the criminals of his day.

The main problem of the criminal is his low self-esteem. This need not be. The voice pronouncing his guilt is loud and clear. He needs to hear another voice reminding him that he is a precious human being with great potential for loving and being loved. Will you be that voice? We need to take responsibility for the labels put on people because they will probably live up to them.

Most criminals are seen through the lens of their crime. Our preoccupation with the what, when, where, and how of crime, and not the why, allows us as a community not to look at ourselves, not to see what produces crime among us, to avoid becoming aware of our common participation in evil. It's not just the criminal and victim who are on trial here. We all are. Crime doesn't just come out of the blue. We scapegoat all the time, and most of the time we don't care because the people we do it to are not important enough to cause us to go through the painful process of realizing that what we are doing is unjust and is preventing us from looking at what we need to do to reduce crime.

Most of us have committed some crime. Usually it's been minor, or exploratory, or temporary, or easily hid. Like a rich man cheating on his income tax, or a distraught mother who loses control, or a youth who experiments a little with drugs, or an adolescent who occasionally has homosexual relations—the behavior is hardly noticed. Others do not think the person doing it is a criminal. But if a powerful person or the police should get involved, they may get labeled a nut, whore, queer, crook, drug addict. Then watch out.

The punishment model is based on finding someone to blame so the rest of us can get off the hook. It focuses on labeling, blaming, and punishing. It doesn't ask why did this happen? It doesn't look at the whole picture of what happened here to cause this situation. It leaves many questions unanswered and not even asked. The total truth needs to come out. Each party needs to be heard and listened to. The atmosphere of looking at the problem needs to be non-threatening in order to get at the truth. Otherwise, the fear of punishment will prevent the truth from coming out. The opposite of the punishment model is the reconciliation model. This does not let anyone off the hook. We must all take responsibility for the problem.

In the Bible, there are stories that have to do with labels. A person's name was changed by God to give them a new identity. The change of a name usually meant a change in the path of life they were taking. There was a man named Jacob. The name "Jacob" means cheat. Jacob cheated his brother. He lived up to his name. But one time in a crisis situation he faced God. Here is the really strange thing. When God said to Jacob. "And, I will bless you," God went on to ask, "What is your name?" "My name is Jacob [or cheat]." And God said, "Your name is no longer Jacob. It's Israel. You have become a prince. That is your real name: 'Prince.'" And the amazing thing was this man became a prince of God. Because God called him by his rightful name, he became what he was called.

People often behave the way they do because of the name we force on them, consciously or unconsciously. But people often change as a result of being given a new name. Sometimes when people visit prison and meet some of the residents there, they look at them not as fellow human beings but as criminals, as something less than they are. They wonder, *Is this guy a rapist, a murderer, or a bank robber?* Now these people in prison are people who are our brothers and sisters, members of our own family. They are just struggling as the rest of us on the sea of life. They are no different than we are; they are humans just like us.

Changing Labels

The greatest need the criminal has is for a good friend who accepts him as a human being who has a problem. The criminal's problems include substance abuse, dysfunctional families, domestic violence, poverty, unemployment, illiteracy, and mental illness, etc. Getting involved is not reacting to the problem but helping with the problem. The criminal needs a new name, a new self-concept. You can help by not reinforcing a person's destructive self-concept.

Chapter 3
THE MOST IMPORTANT GIFT YOU CAN GIVE ANYONE

This chapter has been included because many of us suffer from poor self- esteem. Self-esteem has to do with how you see yourself and not necessarily with the real you. You may see yourself in a positive or negative way. If positive then you say to yourself, "I can do it. I like myself." If negative you say to yourself, "I can't do it. I am no good. I don't like myself." Sometimes negatives are related to a person's physical characteristics. "I don't like how I look. I'm too tall or too short, or my feet are too big or too small. I'm too fat or too thin." Sometimes negatives are related to a person's intelligence. "I am not very smart. I am stupid." It represents dissatisfaction with how you see yourself. In other words, you are not happy and positive with your image, and therefore you won't be successful. Your potential will never be realized because of your poor self-image.

The Bible says, "As a man thinks in his heart so he is." In other words what we think of ourselves is very important. What we think of ourselves determines what we will be like. It becomes a self-fulfilling prophecy. This speaks of the power of your mind over your personality. If your mind contains good, positive, happy thoughts, you will project good happy positive thoughts through your life.

Some people when asked, "How are you today?" always answer, "Great, fantastic, marvelous, top drawer," or something like it. You know what? That's how they appear to others. What they say they become.

This can work for you as well. Why not give it a try? Don't minimize the power of your mind. You have heard of placebos used in medical research. A certain new medicine was given to a group of people; another similar group was given a placebo. The placebo was just sugar. It had no chemical effect, but it did have a positive psychological effect. Years ago vitamin C was given to a group of people to see if they would benefit by having fewer colds. A similar group received a placebo. The group receiving a placebo had fewer colds, not the group receiving vitamin C, showing the power of your mind over your body. Physicians often prescribe placebos to patients who would benefit from a psychological boost. People believe it will work and it does.

Low self-esteem results in people who lack confidence in their abilities. They think because they failed once they will fail again. Their failure was a painful experience, so they don't want to fail again and won't even try. People with low self-esteem have an idea things just happen to them. They think they don't make things happen themselves; yet nothing could be further from the truth. You cause things to happen. You can make things happen. Often people make little effort to get what they would like because they lack self-confidence. Such people will never have happy lives because other people don't like to be around negative people. Negative people don't inspire other people because of their depressed and depressing outlook.

Some people have been taught not to like themselves. Their parents have told them they are stupid, clumsy, and can't do anything right. Even your school system reinforces your poor self-image. The way we grade children is a form of abuse. In schools, try as they might, some can't keep up and often quit trying. The influence of teachers goes beyond belief. Children spend more time with teachers than anyone else in their lives. A good teacher is worth his/her weight in gold. Unfortunate is the child who ends up with a poor teacher.

Other people often contribute to people's poor self-image by labeling them. Crown attorneys and your correctional system label them. Of course, they begin to think of themselves as different and misfits, since they can't keep up with those in the mainstream. They will find another family like themselves who have trouble fitting into the mainstream. People who have trouble fitting in often end up in the criminal world.

Let me ask you a personal question. What do you think of yourself? Now be honest. Can you say, "I am happy with myself"? How is your success in life? Do you think of yourself as great, wonderful, successful? You can think this way. You may need to change your self-concept, or how you see yourself. Believe me, you can be a healthy, happy and successful person.

The first thing in changing your thinking involves deciding to do it. Like other things in life for you to be firm in a resolution, you need good reasons to back up your decision. This will make it possible to see your decision through. One positive result of changing your thinking will be a change in your feelings and actions. Universal laws like this don't change. Change your thinking and you will change yourself. Henry Ford said, "If you think you can do a thing or think, you can't do a thing,your right."

We have all been created equal and different. Everyone has a mission, and everyone has their own mission. We have different gifts for our mission, and different handicaps to overcome. Face your handicap and rise above it. Examples of people who have risen above their handicaps are on every hand today. You can, too. God has given you a mission. Use the gifts you have been given to fulfill your mission.

You need self-love and self-acceptance in order to have a happy, healthy, and successful life, otherwise your guilt and fear will cripple you the rest of your life. Your past has to be put to rest in order to move ahead, otherwise you will spin your wheels the rest of your life. Your answer to guilt and fear is an experience with Jesus Christ (God). Many people have sought God and found him to be alive and well. You can do the same. It's up to you. God can wipe out your past and clean your slate. An experience with the living God will give you self-esteem and you will discover you belong to God and that God doesn't make any junk. It will give you power and strength to overcome your handicap. You can move on and have a healthy, happy, and successful life. Once a blind man was brought to Jesus for healing. His problem was obvious; he could not see. Jesus, seeing his problem restored his sight. Jesus does a similar thing for everyone who comes to him. If guilt and fear drag you down, Jesus will take care of those things and give you a new self-image. Then, you can join the blind man who said after his healing, "Once I was blind but now I see."

Chapter 17 of this book deals in detail with having an encounter with your living God. There you will also learn how meditation and prayer can help. For now, here are a few practical steps to take to build your self-esteem.

21

Feed your mind the right diet. You have already started this. Right now you are reading a book that can make a tremendous difference in your life. If you are not a reader, then listen to your television and radio for programs that deal with material like you find in this book. Good self-esteem is not a lifetime gift. Self- esteem needs to be fed throughout one's life.

You need to set goals for every day. Ask yourself every night, "What am I going to do tomorrow morning? What am I going to do tomorrow afternoon? What am I going to do tomorrow evening?" If you are not already doing this, make it a rule for living your life, starting today.

Our friends have a great influence on us. In our early years, parents had a great influence. As we grew, our friends gained more and more influence. You have experienced the influence of many other people in your life. If they were polite and kind, you will be polite and kind. If their language was good, your language will be good. If, on the other hand, their behavior was impolite and unkind, you will be the same. Your friends will influence you to be like them, so be careful in your choice of friends since you will become like them. Positive people produce positive people, and negative people produce negative people.

Positive affirmations should make you and others feel good. They need to be said three to five times every day, and it's best to say them out loud. They will affect your way of thinking, feeling, and acting. Saying, "I love myself," will have an effect on you. It will change you. When you answer a phone and someone asks, "How are you today?" saying to them, "Great, fantastic, marvelous," will help you and them. Now because this response sounds different than your usual response, it will seem strange at first. Positive thoughts stamped on your brain time and time again will have a positive effect on you, as well as on others. Small wonder negative thinking characterizes so many people when negative thoughts swirl around us all the time. This practice of repeating positive affirmations needs to be another rule for living your life.

One final word on self-esteem: You must take action. Set your goals. Now get going. Don't be afraid to push yourself.

Besides labeling and resulting poor self image there are a number of problem areas related to relationships that people need to deal with in order to have healthy, happy, successful lives. Chapters 4 to12 will deal with these problem areas.

Chapter 4
HOW TO MAKE A GOOD MARRIAGE BETTER

You have just begun your marriage. You will be working on your relationship as long as you're married. It is your commitment that holds your relationship together. The Bible presents it as a "one flesh" idea saying, "The two shall be joined together and become one flesh." It is the commitment that keeps people together when things are going good or bad.

All relationships have their ups and downs, so expect them. Every one falls in and out of love on a regular basis. You have two very different people coming together in a relationship who have been raised in different situations. One has brothers and sisters, and the other was raised as an only child. They have been born with different genes. One likes chocolate ice cream, and one likes vanilla. You must agree to disagree and go right on loving each other in spite of your differences.

Husbands and wives are very different. Often when counseling a couple, I give them a test to show them how they are different. They are very surprised by their differences and say, "I can't believe you thought that." If you remind yourself you had different parents, different brothers and sisters, and different everything, you can see why in a relationship you need to allow for your differences. You can't afford to get upset because your spouse doesn't see things like you do. Relax, they never will, so grow up and let them be different. You need to adjust to your partner, who is continually changing. Your partner has changed a great deal since you married. This can be very upsetting at times, but recognizing your situation helps you cope with it. The good thing is you can always be learning something different about your mate.

A relationship requires communication. When a couple stops communicating because of problems, watch for storm clouds to break. We must not allow our differences to stop our communication. The elderly couple had just returned from a visit at their neighbor's house. It was bedtime. As their habit was, the wife took out some bread she had just baked, cut off the crust, and gave it to her husband of fifty years. She had been doing this since they were married. Well this was the night. He blew his stack, as he said, "Not the crust again. You always give me the crust which I hate." To which she replied, "I give you the crust of bread because it's the best part of the bread. The part I really like." For a relationship to exist there must be communication. Someone sends a message, and someone else receives it. This involves a receiver sending and a sender receiving and so on and on it goes, back and forth.

A wife was asked what do you expect from your husband? Her answer was just three words: "acceptance, kindness, and listening." She wanted acceptance as a unique person, just as she was, the good and bad. We are all like her. Perfection escapes all humans. A very wise man once said, "When my wife's hard for me to love and accept, she needs my acceptance and love the most." The second thing this wife wanted was kindness. Kindness must characterize the close relationship of marriage. After counseling sessions, my parting words to many couples whose marriages were falling apart were, "Be kind to one another." There was so much unkindness going on in these marriages. The third thing this wife wanted was a spouse who would listen to her. I don't mean a spouse who lets themselves be bossed around, but a spouse who is an active listener. Most husbands would be happy to receive from their wives these same three things: acceptance. kindness and a listening ear.

Let's look at the difference between romantic love and what the Bible calls *agape* love. Romantic love is fantastic. Jim and Jane meet. Wham! Wow! it's magical! Something happens between them. It's in their eyes. It's a beautiful day. They are out sailing. A storm comes up suddenly, and they get soaked to the skin but afterwards they talk of this boat ride as being so awesome. A few years later they recall it as that awful day in the sailboat when it poured. We read in the Bible that Jacob worked seven years for Rachel. It seemed like a day to him. Seven years were like one day. Wow! That's romantic love. You don't control romantic love, it controls you. Unfortunately, as time passes, instead of saying, "You are so wonderful," we start saying, "The trouble with you is…"

Agape love on the other hand is a commitment to love. It is something you do. Something you control. It is described in the Bible as being patient, kind, not rude, not proud, keeping no record of wrong, not easily angered, and permanent. When I see pictures of our soldiers return to their spouses with no legs or arms, terribly disfigured, sexually impotent, I wonder how the relationship will go. Will the spouse be able to accept him/her as they are now? Agape love says, "yes." Agape love is unconditional. You accept the other person no matter what.

Don't get me wrong, God has given us a wonderful gift in romantic love, including sex. Without it we might not have children. It certainly draws our young people together. Mature love is described in the Bible as a love that grows as the years go by. A good relationship will involve both romantic and mature love.

You and your spouse need to take responsibility for the relationship. The word "partnership" best describes a marriage. Spouses often blame each other. It is common to hear each say, "The trouble with you is so and so." For a relationship to be successful, both need to work on it. If trouble arises, the problem is not the husband or wife but the relationship. Blaming will get you nowhere. Each spouse has to ask, "What can I do to make this a better relationship?" Focus your mind on the positive. Give your partner positive affirmations, such as, "I like you because of so and so." Kindness is basic in a healthy relationship. Be kind for Jesus' sake.

Be sure to keep in mind you are both different and changing all the time. Neither of you are the same as when you married. Adjusting to changes over time must be expected.

You need to manage your time so you and your spouse spend some quality time together. Your relationship must be worked on continuously in order to thrive. Without time together, you will grow apart. If you are raising children, you must be consistent with your discipline. To do this you must discuss Junior's situation. You also need to have some fun together in order to keep the fire burning.

A relationship grows by working on it. This involves being together and sharing. You need to get to know each other by sharing your history, feelings, and understanding. Here's a warning about sharing. Don't push your partner, only share what you're comfortable sharing at this time in the relationship. Sometimes it is better not to share some things. Something that will hurt your partner should not be shared. As time goes on there will be tough times. Maybe a serious ailment will be faced by you or your spouse. Try to put yourself in your spouse's place. Listen to what your spouse wants to share and encourage him or her to have hope and believe in the goodness of God. Every crisis gives you an opportunity to grow your relationship.

Your relationship is an equal partnership. You must not try to control your partner. You must learn to negotiate and compromise in a relationship because of your differences. Someone said, "If two people agree all the time, one must be doing all the thinking." You will find it best to divide up your areas of responsibility. The one who is best at finance will take care of that area and so on. What you are good at you want to do. Things need to be worked out. A healthy relationship has no place for intimidation or controlling the other person with put-downs. Because you have agreed to disagree in your relationship and go right on loving each other, you will be able to share your ideas in an open manner.

Positive affirmation characterizes healthy relationships. Negativism characterizes troubled relationships. When people are getting married,

they see their future partner as being wonderful. After a while you hear them saying, "The trouble with my wife or my husband is…" Then you know the honeymoon is over. Can you turn a negative relationship around? Yes, by affirming your partner. Think of the good things about your partner. You might be surprised how many there are. Tell them what you like about them, and you will find they begin to change. And you begin to change.
I'm not suggesting you be dishonest in order to manipulate another person. No! Be honest, there are many good things about your partner. Your affirmation will make your partner feel better about themselves, and because they feel better they will act better. It builds their self-esteem, and that's a good thing in relationships.

In the next chapter we will look at how some other problems must be faced in order to have a really good relationship.

Chapter 5
THE KEY TO A SUCCESSFUL RELATIONSHIP

In the beginning God saw it was not good for man to be alone. He needed a companion, a friend like himself. So marriage is a close friendship. I want to say three things about the kind of friendship I see in a successful marriage.

We share things that are happening in our lives. My wife Joan and I have been going on a date at least once a week for years. This may be just to a doughnut shop for coffee. Our lives have always been very busy with both of us working and raising five children, but we need a time to be alone together. Every couple needs time together to share what's going on in their life. Sometimes we don't talk for a while, but we are together. The other night I saw a beautiful sunset.
I called to Joan, "Come have a look at this sunset." The clouds and colors were so unusual. Joan came, took a look, and agreed it was beautiful and so different. Now if she had said, "You're stupid; I don't like sunsets," I would have felt bad. However, she shared in my experience, and it made me feel good. How do you do in this area of sharing experiences with your mate?. When your wife tells you she saw this or did this, do you listen and support her in what she 's experiencing? Companionship involves a sharing of experiences.

Companionship also involves a sharing of feelings. There's place for openness, a sharing of feelings. We need to feel we are accepted by our partner with our feelings. Unless you share how you feel your partner will never get to know you. Ken said, "We never talk about our feelings, they're not something you talk about." Helen said, "Feelings were never talked about in my family— never." However, I'm warning you to be careful when it comes to sharing feelings. If they will hurt your partner, better not share them.

A final area to share as good friends is understanding. Being good friends means you have someone who supports you, listens to you, and understands you. Many of us have a problem listening, finding a time to listen, making a time to listen. If you have been apart for a while and you come together, you both have something you want to share. The wife thinks of things that have happened in her life while they have been separated. The husband does the same. So you both talk at the same time, and no one listens. We hear each other but are not listening. "I'm just waiting for you to stop talking so I can start." To become better friends take time to share your experiences, feelings, and understanding.

It's easy to see why there's conflict in relationships. People are just so different. Someone said, "The family that fights together stays together."

Shocking but true. This conflict doesn't go away after a while. It's there for the entire relationship, so we had better learn how to handle it. How to work it out. A man got up in a group and said he was having trouble with his wife. She would go out without telling him where she was going. He could not find her, and he would get very worried. This man was seventy-two years old and never had this problem before. Conflict shows you're in a relationship. You're not bothered about what your neighbor's wife does because you're not in a relationship with her. Someone said, "Marriage is like two porcupines cuddling together. The closer you get the more prickly it gets." Every room in your home has a potential for conflicts. Take the bathroom. Some believe you should roll the toilet paper over the top of a roll. Others know it should come from the bottom. Conflict is part of marriage.

Example 2   **HOW TO HANDLE CONFLICT**

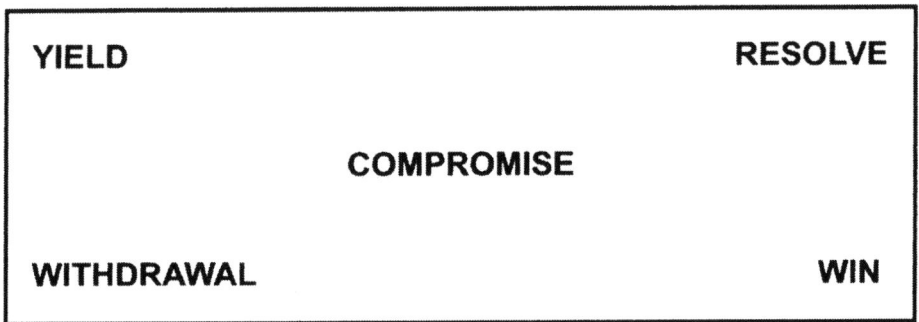

YIELD	**RESOLVE**
COMPROMISE	
WITHDRAWAL	**WIN**

There are many negative ways of handling conflict. These ways must be avoided if possible.

First of these is withdrawal. This may seem okay, but the problem with withdrawal is we're avoiding the relationship. The other day I was counseling a couple and asked each one to tell me the problem from his or her point of view. The wife blasted out her anger over this and that. The husband's comment was, "You never told me that before." That is the problem. We withdraw from the conflict. We don't agree but we hide our disagreement. What do you think is the result of our hiding our thoughts and feelings? It results in a slow-burning anger and shame. Withdrawal from conflict is a poor way to handle it. Sometimes we hear of couples who are filing for divorce, and other people looking on say, "I can't understand it, I've never seen them fight." That's the problem. They keep it in and don't work it out. They have a kind of peace, but underneath there is a volcano ready to erupt and finally it does. As I said before, you can't have a relationship with out conflict

Another way of handling conflict is winning. If you feel you must win at all cost, it's likely your self-concept is being threatened. You must dominate and control others. If you win, you feel good. If you lose, you feel bad. What do you think your spouse feels like when you win? I imagine he or she is angry. Winning, like withdrawing, destroys a relationship.

Still another way to handle conflict negatively is to yield, giving in to get along. You don't like it, but rather than face conflict you yield. How does that make you feel? Not too good, but angry. Maybe angry at yourself for yielding, as well as at the other guy. Yielding is not a good way to handle conflict. So what can we do?

There are positive ways to handle conflict. One of these is to compromise. Here you give a little to get a little. You let up on your demands or ideas a little to help the other person give up a little. The other day, I met with a couple who were arguing over disciplining their son Johnny. It was obvious that by nature one was very strict and one was very lenient. One of them said, "I guess I have been too hard on Johnny. I've expected too much of him." The other said," I've been too easy. Let's get together on how we discipline Johnny." One positive solution for conflict is to compromise, to give a little to get a little.

Another positive way to handle conflict is to resolve it. You look at both sides of an issue in an open and honest way. One may change and accept the views of the other, or you may decide to tolerate the differences. In every relationship we must agree to disagree and still go on loving each other. There is no other way for any relationship to be healthy. Agree to disagree and go on loving and working together.

Every couple needs to have a serious discussion about children because parenting is serious business and very expensive. There are some questions you need to think about. Do both of you want children? How are you going to discipline your children? Are you facing other problems related to children such as step parenting or blended families?

I want to say a word about sex in a relationship. Sex is an important gift God has given us. I don't mention sex to cause anyone discomfort. I believe a marriage is much more than sex. I remember George Burns, a comedian, saying, "A great marriage is not what you do in bed but what you do when you get out of bed." The Bible is clear that sex is not just for having children. Through it people are saying, "I love you, I want you, we are one flesh." The best sex is in marriage.

Poor health can be a problem in a relationship. You were married for better or worse. I hope it turns out to be for better. However, sooner or later, health will be a problem. It may be mental or physical health or both. For instance, depression on the part of either spouse can wreak havoc in a relationship. Fortunately, depression can usually be successfully treated. Other important aspects in a marital relationship, such as sex drive, can be affected by poor health. Both partners need to adjust to this. I hope you will face health problems in a positive manner. Such problems can be seen as an intervention, which can result in positive growth. As I said in a previous paragraph, there is much more to a relationship than sex. More emphasis needs to be put on other things like enjoying being with the other person and sharing in the three areas I mentioned at the beginning of this chapter: experience, feelings, and understanding. I've seen relationships grow tremendously when one partner is not well. It's time for more kindness, tenderness, hugs, and kisses.

Surveys indicate money, not sex, is the main cause of divorce. In a healthy relationship, couples compromise all the time. Compromises need to be worked out in a fair manner. Different couples do this in different ways. For instance, one time the wife gets her choice, the next time the husband gets his choice. Both husband and wife need to be comfortable with the compromise. Problems develop when a husband and wife are not mature enough to work things out. They begin to act like little children, each wanting his or her own way. I hope you're secure enough in your relationship that you can work things out in an open and honest manner.

Here are some things to remember when it comes to money. Expenses should never be more than your income. Buy things your family needs. Plan events for the family that cost little or nothing. You will never have enough money to do all you want or buy everything you want. Be sure to count your many blessings.

Watch out for stressors. Stressors are things that stress you or your spouse and affect your relationship. We all change under stress. We worry needlessly about our relationship when the problem is that one or the other spouse is suffering from stress. When one of you is stressed, check to see what the problem is and deal with it. It could be a health or job issue or some other issue. Hopefully the stress from whatever will pass, and things will be back to normal soon.

What's the best guide ever written for a healthy, happy, successful relationship? I have left the most important thing I want to say on marriage until the end of this chapter. There are those who would tell you that the basic thing in any marriage, the thing which holds it together, is good communication. Not so; it is love as described in 1 Corinthians 13 (Bible). One of the most damaging ideas today is the idea that marriage is held together by romantic love. Now, be careful, I don't want to take romance out of marriage. Romance is part of a marriage but not the most important part, not the part that keeps a marriage and family together. The thing that keeps it together is agape love. We need to be like Betty who left her husband the following note when she went to work. "Bill, I hate what you did this morning. Love, Betty."

Chapter 6
HOW TO BE A GOOD PARENT

Parenting and crime are related. Parenting is never simple or easy. It is very difficult. I know, as I have been a parent to five children. Even with a lot of courses on parenting and reading many books on the subject and teaching parenting groups and counseling parents having problems with their children for years, I still don't know it all. However, there are many things I have learned and will share with you in this chapter.

There was a break-in at a store that sold expensive blue jeans and leather jackets. Two men were involved. They broke a plate glass window and entered the store in a flash. An alarm system went off. They grabbed some piles of blue jeans and as many leather jackets as they could and threw them in their stolen van. As they sped down the street, they met a police cruiser coming toward them with its siren screaming. It sped by them on their way to the blue jean store. The boys had a good laugh over this. They took the goods they had stolen and began to sell them at a reduced price. After a couple weeks, word got out and they were arrested and sentenced to prison. When I visited them in prison they thought this was a great big joke. Where did these young men learn their values? What did they learn from their parents?

You know, it doesn't matter so much what parents say if they contradict what they say by what they do. If children observe that their parents are dishonest and selfish, if Dad admits to the kids that he steals from the government by falsifying his income tax records, or a phone rings and Mother says her husband is out when he's sitting right there—children aren't stupid. They see a contradiction between things they've been taught and their parents' actions. On the other hand, if there's consistency between what parents say and do the result is the children's conscience will bother them when they do those things, they have been taught by word and deed what is wrong. It's said our conscience is the voice of our parents.

A baby's birth though painful is a time of tremendous joy. It's like a miracle taking place before our very eyes. The pregnancy has been long and costly in physical ways, but mother and baby are doing fine. Everyone is joyful, and the baby is so beautiful. We must get a few things ready for the homecoming of mother and baby. Father is relieved and has already begun to plan for the future of his new baby. He has high hopes for the days ahead for his little one. He is going to see that his child gets some of those things he never had but wanted when he was growing up.

When a baby is not accepted by its parents, it's a tragedy. Some babies cry because they are not getting the attention they need. The parents have abandoned them in favor of their own selfish pursuits or desires. The child is crying and sick because it's not loved. The result of such behavior on the part of parents is a life scarred because of the lack of love. All kinds of problems are ahead for a child raised in such a situation. It can result in a difficult personality, problems in school, or even ending up in an institution or prison.

Babies are all different. Some are born handicapped. These handicaps may be mental or physical. Each one will require some learned compensation by the child. Even handicapped children who receive a high level of help may be able to enjoy good lives. Failure to receive the level of help they require will prevent their potential from being reached. To get the care they require, they need advocates in our system. Many parents become excellent advocates. Otherwise, it's hoped others aware of the child's difficulties will get involved.

Good parenting is important. I have worked with hundreds of families and it's clear to me that it's essential for children to have good parenting if they are to enjoy a good life. Children need to learn self-discipline, which they learn by being disciplined and seeing this in the lives of their parents. In most cases, one's work ethic is learned from their parents. We become like our parents. If our parents were hard working, we will be hard working. If our parents helped people in need, we will do the same. Things whether good or bad run in families.

Parents need to sacrifice for their children, As I mentioned, being a parent is costly. Children have many needs and for many years are dependent on their parents. Slowly they move from total dependency to becoming independent. It's the parents' job to guide them through these years of growth. They need good nourishment for their bodies and minds as well as an abundance of love and understanding.

There are two kinds of love I want to draw to your attention. One is unconditional love, and the other is tough love. I said parenting isn't easy or simple. When it comes to tough love and unconditional love, it isn't one or the other but both/and. These are not opposites; both are required.

A child needs to be loved unconditionally in order to be emotionally healthy. Conditional love is not good for children. The idea that "if you do what I want, I will love you, and if you don't, I won't" is wrong. The child needs to know that they are loved no matter what. I have parented five very different children and given each one of them unconditional love. It has resulted in each one of them in their own time becoming a happy, loving person. Sure, they have had their problems, but today they have a good, positive self-concept. They can each say, "I love myself."

What we call tough love has to do with discipline. A child who is loved unconditionally requires discipline. Not to discipline a child results in a monster who wants his way all the time. I said parenting was not easy or simple. Too much pressure on a child at a certain time in their development can result in driving them away, and you lose your opportunity of working with them. A good parent knows his/her child and is the best judge of what is going on with the child. I would also suggest that good parents will get all the help they can from professional counselors.

Sometimes a child's behavior is inappropriate. Some children will need to learn what is appropriate behavior. With some a frown is all that's needed; others will need much more. Inappropriate behavior is being used by the child because of a problem or frustration. It is an indication things are not going well for them. When this is a minor problem, the parent can deal with it through consequences such as a time out or the loss of something the child likes. Other cases of inappropriate behavior will require the help and support of a good family counselor.

When I think of inappropriate behavior, manipulation comes to mind. Manipulation is common to all humans. It is born in us to survive

45

and to get what we want by any means. This is found in all of us to some extent. In my work with criminals, it is common. In order to survive, they have become experts at manipulation. That's why we say, "someone conned me," which means, "they fooled me to get what they wanted."
I believe rather than teaching children to manipulate, which often involves dishonesty, we should encourage them to be open and honest in their communication. This may cause some disagreement and conflict, but this will not hurt.

Good self-esteem is the secret of a happy, successful life. It is feeling good about yourself. Loving yourself is having a positive attitude to self. It says, "I can and I will." It is fed by success and other people, as well as self-talk. It's a gift we can give other people by encouraging them and thanking them for what they are doing for others. It tends to make them happy and healthy. It encourages the best in people. A negative self-image is destructive and has the opposite effect on people. Parents have a great influence on the way a child sees himself or herself. The greatest gift you can give your child is good self-esteem.

We live in an increasingly scary world. There have been many changes in our world in the last fifty years. We have seen a decline in the teaching of what many would call the old-fashioned values such as unselfishness, concern for others, and honesty. As people have moved from rural to urban centers, they have lost many of the values that were taught where people lived in a close-knit community setting. Parents today need to see that their children are taught values by word and deed. For years the church was the center for such teaching. Today many children do not have the benefit of church instruction. With the coming of television and computer, there has been a tremendous change in what values our children are taught. The results of this are seen in an increase in the number and seriousness of the crimes they are committing.

I have worked with juvenile criminals and their families for many years. As a parent how are you to respond to Junior getting into trouble with the law? This is serious but believe me it's not the end of Junior. It's an opportunity for an intervention. Though I have worked in a juvenile institution for young criminals, it's my opinion, if the problem is not too serious, it's better to deal with it outside of an institution if the help is available. Too many parents are fed up with Junior and only too happy to have someone else take responsibility for him so they can get on with their lives. I would suggest you get all the advice you can from professional juvenile counselors. Most communities offer help and support for parents. Also don't forget, this too will pass. Many young people have benefited from getting into trouble with the police, even at a very early age.

Like most things, I believe discipline is taught to children by word and example. If parents are disciplined, their children are likely to be the same. Discipline is necessary to have any degree of success in our world. We live in a world run by the clock, and we must learn to show up on time. Some of us need to learn that the boss calls the shots as well. This is important in school and on the job. I have known some parents who thought that disciplining their child was not kind. The opposite is the truth. Not to discipline a child is unkind. In order to grow up to be a happy, successful adult one needs to learn to be disciplined. It's very important. Children will learn discipline not only by being disciplined but also by the parents' example of a disciplined life. Discipline is the kind thing to teach a child. Remember, "Train up a child in the way he should go and he will not depart from it when he is old" (Bible).

From time to time some children will require punishment. This is not a happy situation for the child or parent, but the duty of a good parent. The child has a lesson to learn. Today punishment is done by denying some privilege, for instance, going to a movie or watching a favorite television program. Careful thought needs to be given to the degree of punishment. Punishment should not be given while one is emotionally upset. Too often a parent threatens some terrible consequence only to lessen the consequence when they cool down. Better to deal with the situation in a sane, thoughtful manner. This reaction of the parent will be a good model for the child to follow when he or she gets upset.

Parents need to be on the same page when raising their children. It's not unusual for children to use their parents as pawns to get their own way. If the parents are not openly talking about Junior and what is happening in his life, they will find they're having problems concerning Junior's discipline. Parents need to continually keep in touch with each other concerning Junior's requests and any disciplinary measures they have taken. They need to work out with each other their common stand concerning Junior's behavior, otherwise the home is not going to be as happy a place as it should be.

Parents must be good role models of what they teach their children. Their teaching isn't going to do much good unless it's being modeled by what they are doing. For instance, Junior is making a racket upstairs and Dad is getting madder and madder. Finally, Dad not only calls upstairs for him to quiet down but yells at the top of his lungs for him to shut up. Do you see the contradiction? We must always try to model what we're trying to teach. Most of us have models we would like to imitate. Who they are is very important, for you are apt to reflect that person in many ways.

Chapter 7
PARENTING DIFFICULT CHILDREN

Children are not born equal. That does not mean that some are better or worse than others are, but it does mean they are different. Children learn in different ways and at different speeds. Some children have a difficult time adjusting to their environment. If parents do not recognize this fact, the road ahead will be rough. This chapter is included because some families find it difficult to cope. Here are a number of helpful tips. I have worked with families of special children for years and have found there are some things you can do to make your family situation much more tolerable for everyone. I have included here a number of helpful ideas.

These children look the same but learn differently than the average. They have a difficult time coping. This is a handicap, and if not recognized it will result in poor self-esteem and problems relating in your family and community,

The symptoms of the children I am dealing with in this chapter would include the following. An attention problem, which results in them not hearing all you say, forgetting what you said they were to do. Another symptom is being impulsive. They don't think before they act, forgetting the consequences of their actions. Typically these children are more active and get into more things than your average child. Another common symptom is they don't take direct orders from an adult well. It's easy to see why these children are difficult to deal with.

How you treat your difficult child is very important. Do you treat him warmly with lots of hugs and kisses, or do you wonder what he's into now? Is your relationship negative or positive? If it's negative, you need to do everything you can to turn it around. Difficult children respond poorly to the negative. I am not suggesting you give in to the whims of your child. I am saying your times together for the most part need to be happy, fun times. Thank God for your child. Your child is a precious gift from God and will bring a blessing to your life.

The Bible gives us the right emphasis in regards to parenting when it says, "Train up a child in the way he shall go and he will not depart from it when he is old." Without training we are just one generation from becoming pigs. Your child needs to be trained by you from his/her birth to be a responsible, happy, and disciplined person. These three things, responsibility, happiness, and discipline, are necessary for one to have the best life possible.

It's important for you to be a thinking and not a reacting parent. We are great imitators. If I put on a mad face and yell at my child, my child is apt to put on a mad face and yell at me. You have heard of monkey see, monkey do. When you get mad and look mad and yell at Junior, Junior is apt to copy you. Remember monkey see, monkey do. When we get angry with someone, they in turn get angry at us. In your home, this results in chaos. People are angry and hurt. There's a better way to deal with situations than reacting. You need to think about what has happened and the best way to handle your situation. What will give you the results you are seeking? Remember, with difficult children positive reinforcement of good behavior will go much further to change the behavior than negative reinforcement of bad.

The reason difficult children have a problem with acceptable behavior is because of the frustration in their lives. Often the expectations set are far too high for them. In school they are expected to do as well as their brother who got straight As. This is impossible for them so pressure is put on. The pressure is negative, and the result is negative behavior on their part. Mother or Dad wanted Junior to be a doctor or a lawyer. Unfortunately, Junior has been given only two cylinders and they are none too good. We need to learn to accept and love people as they are, not as we wish they were. Lower expectations will often result in a healthier, happier child.

If you want to change your child's behavior use positive reinforcement. Parents using negative reinforcement with difficult children find it doesn't work. Forget the negative. Find something your child does well and be sure to praise and reward him in some way. He will learn to do what you want a lot quicker if you do this. All children need to be taught to honor boundaries. There's a right way to act. When a child recognizes and watches the boundaries, they receive positive reinforcement. They will quickly learn to do the things the way they should. They need to receive the attention they crave not by being bad but by being good. With a little thought and practice, you can improve your home situation a great deal. Your home will be a much happier place for all.

You decide what's appropriate behavior for your child. Pay attention to the directions given your child and the best way to communicate directions. Change your method if need be so your child understands. Be consistent in the way you deal with things so you are not confusing your child. Directions must be clear and consistent. You modify your behavior in order to modify that of your child. You must promote positive behavior.

Many of these children get in trouble with the police. Their handicap favors this happening. If they end up in a juvenile detention center, things are apt to go from bad to worse. There's no doubt in my mind that for many in difficulty, the juvenile detention center is the door to a life of crime. I first met Junior in the youth center. Three years later I met him in a medium-security prison, and a few years later he had graduated to a maximum security penitentiary. This pattern is not uncommon.

You need to take care of yourself so you can take care of your child. If you are not good yourself, you are not good for others. You need to have a break from time to time. You need some contact with other adults as well. Watch your mental and physical health. A person will always do a better job with a difficult situation if they are healthy. Do something you enjoy doing from time to time every day. You need to be at your best to handle your situation.

Your child needs positive focused attention. Spend time just loving your child. Listen to what your child has to say. Building a feeling relationship between you and your child is important. This is a happy fun time.

One further tip I have for you is Grandma's rule, which is simple. Here it is, "Do what I want first, and then you can do what you want." Keep it simple, by working on one behavior at a time. Instructions and consequences must be clearly stated. If you say to your child, "Would you like to tidy your bedroom?" or "Do me a favor and tidy your bedroom," I think I know what the answer would be. Say rather, "Please tidy your bedroom before you go out to play." Say it kindly and positively with a smile on your face. Don't give a complex command. Keep them simple and within the capability of your child.

Let me conclude this chapter with this illustration. My friend who is in his fifties told me the other day that he believed he had finally matured. He had been raised by his mother. They were poor, but his mother did the best she could. However, she had her own drug problem. He told me of an incident that happened when he was ten years old. Mother got mad at him one day and told him she wished she had flushed him down the toilet when he was born. This cut him to the core and reinforced his already poor self-esteem. He did poorly in school, making it to grade two. In his teens, he became a drug addict and to make money for drugs he stole. As a result, he was in and out of prison for many years. Finally, he learned he was a child of God and began to like himself. Now at fifty years of age, he has begun to take responsibility for his choices and become a productive citizen. I have heard this kind of story over and over again. Remember, the greatest gift you can give your child is good self-esteem. Poor self-esteem is destructive and the road to hell on earth.

There are two things I want to say in closing this chapter. First, God loves the child with difficulties just as much as the child without such difficulties.

In God's eyes the child who receives Ds at school and who has many difficulties has as much worth as a child who receives straight As and has few difficulties. I would urge you to accept God's view of your child. The second thing I would say is that God has entrusted you with a very special child. Really it's his child, and he has told you "to train him in the way he should go." That is not an easy task and can only be done with God's help.

Chapter 8
ALL ABOUT ADDICTIVE BEHAVIOR

Today there are many types of addictions. For many years the words, "addict" and "addiction"" were applied to those with an alcohol problem. Today we use the word addiction to refer to many different substances and activities. These include drugs, whether they are prescription or illegal, as well as gambling, criminal behavior, and sex. The word addiction is used for something that is destructive to a person's wellbeing. Some use the word in reference to things like smoking, coffee, food, and sweets, behaviors used to comfort one. This book uses it in reference to something people cannot or will not stop using even though it is destroying them.

There are many side effects related to addictions. People steal and kill to support their addiction. Addictions often result in people withdrawing from other people and going into their own shell to cuddle their beloved addiction. The overwhelming desire for whatever they are addicted to and the cost involved leads to all kinds of anti-social behavior such as manipulation, stealing, cheating and anger. Left untreated, the result of the addiction can be insanity and death.

The effects of drug abuse, including alcohol, are more obvious than other addictions. The effects of an alcoholic's behavior on the family are legion. There are continual quarrels about drinking. Inhibitions are blurred resulting in physical abuse. In the lives of alcoholics, there is a history of divorce. The children are afraid to bring their friends home because Daddy's behavior is erratic. The children's behavior at school and in the community is often inappropriate. Frequently we have signs of fetal alcohol syndrome in the children. Financial problems are common. People are uptight, fearful, and uncertain as to what will happen next. To the community and workplace, the alcoholic leaves an example of a messed up life, inappropriate behavior, and a hateful memory.

Many things contribute to becoming an addict. For some, it is the friends they keep. You can tell a person by their friends. If you hang around a drinking crowd you will likely drink. For others, they were raised in the environment. If your parents were alcoholics, there is a chance that you will follow their example. For others, it is their drug of choice for self-medication. Whatever their problem—worry, fear, anger, depression—alcohol is their medicine of choice. It will help! Heredity and environment have an effect on our addictions. Studies show that children of alcoholics are more likely to have an alcohol problem.

It does not make sense to hang around people who are drinking or indulging in your addiction if you are trying to break the habit. You need to associate with people whose conduct is what you desire for yourself. Models are very important to all of us. We become like the friends we keep and the people we admire.

What can you do to help the addict? One thing you must not do is preach. The addict has heard enough sermons to last them a lifetime. They have heard all about the evils of their addiction. Certainly, you can pray for them and their loved ones. You can be a good friend who will listen to them. Active listening helps people think through their problem. If they are asking for help, do all you can to assistant them. Many people watch what they say and do realizing the importance of their example on those who are enslaved by their habits.

Support groups have proven to be very helpful for many people with addictions. Of the addiction groups, Alcohol Anonymous with its 12-step program is the most famous. The best brief description of AA is contained in the two-paragraph definition that is read at many group meetings. "Alcoholics Anonymous is a fellowship of men and women who share their experience, strength and hope with each other that they may solve their common problem and help others to recover from alcoholism. The only requirement for membership is a desire to stop drinking. There are no dues or fees for AA membership. AA groups are self-supporting through our own contributions. AA is not allied with any sect, denomination, politics, organization or institution; does not wish to engage in any controversy, neither endorses nor opposes any causes. Our primary purpose is to stay sober and help other alcoholics achieve sobriety." Their focus has remained the same since their founding in 1935 and is undoubtedly the reason for their great success.

Different groups for chemical addictions of many types use the 12-step AA program. Groups like Adult Children of Alcoholics, Recovering Couples Anonymous, Al-Anon, Alateen, and many sex and gambling groups, etc., use it. Such groups offer friendship, a knowledge base, and social interaction with people who face a similar problem. As addictions are not cured, it is easy to slip back into them. Many who have met with success through a program find it helpful to have a group available for a tune up at some future time when life has not been treating them very well.

Highlights of a 12-step program included the following:

1. Emphasis on honesty. This honesty involves admittance that people have no power over their addictions.
2. Turning from self to God. They come to believe that they need to turn themselves

over to God, as they understand him, for help. They realize that it cannot be done on their own.
3. Decision to change. There is a desire to change that results in one becoming less self-centered and more concerned with helping others.

The fifth step in the 12-step program is the biggest step. It is for those who are serious about changing. It is an inventory step. It is a sharing of one's sins with a person who they can trust. This is a very important step. It is a spiritual experience. It is very difficult. It may cause one to cry. They read their inventory, which includes the following:

1. Resentments: This would include the people you are angry with and have not forgiven. You need to write their names down.
2. Fears: This list could include the following: disapproval, pain, failure, success, disappointing someone, being alone, getting sick, dying, being wrong, abandonment, rejection, authority.
3. Sex Problems: This would include unhealthy sexual relationships and how you have hurt people sexually. Include their names.

It is effective to burn what the person has written. The material they want to get rid of is now gone and they can move on. This has been a listening session.

The slate has been wiped clean. We can now move on with our new life of power over our addiction. We are now ready to work with God in removing our character defects. Our new life will include making amends to those we have harmed when it will not hurt them. In addition, through prayer and meditation we will improve our consciousness of God. Our knowledge of God's will and power will increase. We will carry this message to others. The role of a sponsor is important. When new to the group you are sponsored; as time goes on you become a sponsor of others.

As successful as groups are, people are unique. They achieve victory over their addictions in different ways. Their success is what is important.

Some people have had their eyes suddenly opened to the seriousness of their addiction. They believe that either they or someone else is going to be killed because of their addiction. Right there and then they quit.

Individual counseling has helped many get their heads on straight. The counselor uses active listening to assist the person in working through their problem themselves by asking them appropriate questions. The relationship with a counselor gives a person hope that they can find some answers. The counselor provides some understanding of the problem and some ideas of things other people facing the same problem have found helpful. The fact of returning for future visits with the counselor is encouraged and helps people practice what they have learned between sessions. It is also a check on their practice and progress.

The recovery program of the Gamblers Anonymous is based on the 12-step program of alcohol anonymous. They believe that gambling for certain people is an illness called "compulsive gambling." They claim that there is an alternative to the destruction of compulsive gambling, and this alternative is found in their program. Their ranks are filled with members who have recovered from the illness by stopping gambling and attaining a normal way of life. These members are ready to help any individual who passes through their door. The best recommendation for their programming is that it works.

A very serious addiction that needs attention is the use of solvents. Solvents are the drugs of choice for some children and young people. They include airplane glue, nail polish remover, lighter fluid, cleaning fluids, anesthetics, and gasoline. They are taken by putting them on a cloth or in a bag and breathing them. They result in disorientation, exhilaration, and mild intoxication. The effects are short-lived unless one continues to inhale the solvent. The effects include fighting, lighting fires, and dangerous actions like flying off a roof.

For the sex addict, sex has become central in his life. He is completely preoccupied with thoughts of sex and like other addicts denies that he has a problem. He does not believe that he is worthwhile. One of the best-proven paths for the sex addict is the 12-step program of Alcoholics Anonymous. The program helps restore the network of relationships. The addict admits his powerlessness. Values and priorities are reclaimed. He becomes a spiritual human being again and has value. The sex addict needs to take responsibility for his behavior. Sexual desire is a master that can destroy you if you let it. The choice to master rather than serve it is difficult but possible. The key to success is to take responsibility and quit blaming others. A person needs to develop a relapse prevention plan and increase sympathy for others who may be victims of his/her addiction, whether family members or others in the community.

Addicts are all different. Many parents feel that their children should learn to drink moderately so they do not have a problem in drinking too much. However, the first bottle of beer launches some people on the road to addiction. No one knows who has an addictive personality. Some think that beer is not a drug, but of course it is. No one wants to become an addict but many do. All addicts choose to use a drug in the first place.

Chapter 9
EIGHT STEPS FOR GETTING YOUR HEAD ON STRAIGHT

Here are eight steps for getting your head on straight. These steps have proven helpful in changing the behavior of many addicts. They apply to alcohol or any other addictive behavior.

Step 1. Need for an Intervention
You tend to go on your merry way, or not so merry way, until something intervenes. It could be some catastrophe, a terminal illness, or the death of a loved one. It may be a slow realization that there must be more to life than you are presently enjoying. It could be an intervention by a group of concerned friends who are concerned by your bad behavior and its affect. Therefore, they get together and confront you. This type of group intervention has proven to be effective. Other times it may be an intervention by a concerned friend. Something happens to stop your headlong plunge into complete self- destruction.

Step 2. Need to Admit the Problem
You need to admit that you have a problem if you are to take responsibility and do something about it. It is normal to minimize your problem by denying it, when you are already suffering from low self-esteem. However, the open sharing of your problem is the beginning of your recovery.

This is essential. By admitting your problem, you are united with others in the cause of overcoming your addiction, thus working on your recovery. Your addiction is still there but you are doing something definite about it. This gives you some self-esteem. You are already feeling much better.

Step 3. Need for an Experience with God
This is a spiritual experience when you sense the presence of the living God in your life. You are now connected to a higher power. You feel that God accepts you as you are. Your sins have been forgiven. You are now okay. Your self-esteem gets a boost, and now you can be a healthy, happy, successful person. Just as people are different, this experience is different for every person. Up to now, you have tried to overcome your addiction on your own. The Bible says that God is still alive and at work in the lives of people who turn to him. Like many others, you have turned your life over to God and our trusting him for your future.

Step 4. Need for Positive Self-Talk
There is real value in self-talk. It makes a big difference whether one says, "I can," or "I cannot." You make a choice. You need to substitute negative self-talk with positive self-talk. Often when facing a scary situation like a job interview or an appointment with your doctor to get results of your medical test, you are filled with fear. You are worried. You are negative. However, you have a choice. You can be positive. In such a

situation you can say, "I can do all things through Christ who strengthens me." Think about it. You have asked for God's help, and he says he will give you help. Guess what? He does. You find you can get through that difficult situation. A friend said to me the other day that a big change had taken place in his life when he began to say to himself, "I love myself," instead of thinking poorly of himself. Here is an experiment for you to try. Every time you find yourself worrying say to yourself, "I love myself; I really love myself." Your worry is replaced with something positive. Worry is always negative. Replace it with something positive and begin to really live. Here are some statements you can use. Choose two you like and be sure to use them three times a day. "My opinion counts because I am somebody." "It's okay to be selfish sometimes." "It's okay to be me." "I can say no and set boundaries." "I can grow and change even if it means rocking the boat."

Step 5. Need to Break the Cycle of Addiction
You can break your cycle of addiction through substitution. We have just looked at substituting negative thoughts with positive thoughts. This same practice of substitution will break the cycle of addictive behavior as well. When Mary's husband goes to work, she has a shower, then lies down on the bed, and watches a soap. She begins to rub her body and continues until her addiction is temporarily satisfied. Mary needs to break her cycle by changing it. So after her

husband leaves for work, she goes for a long walk. When she gets home, she gets on with the day's chores. With commitment to change and some creative thought, people can break their cycle of addiction.

Step 6. Need for a Positive Role Model
Let me ask you a question. Who is your mentor? Whom would you like to be like? If a good friend dies suddenly and you need some advice, is there someone you could go to? Is there someone you really trust? We tend to copy other people. You may have more than one model in mind. You could be muscular like Fred, or good at solving problems like John. It is a good idea to turn to others for ideas and support. A big part of the success of a group like Alcoholic Anonymous is due to the sponsorship part of its program. Everyone in the program has someone to help and support them. It is good for your mental health to be open with others. Those who keep it all inside are apt to explode some day, or at least have a nervous breakdown.

Step 7. Need to Be a Role Model
Drug abuse is not new. Most cultures have had their drugs for a long time. What is new today is the use of drugs by our young people and the number using them. Drug use among young people is a universal health problem. Society has more pills for more ills than ever before. With

our young people, adolescence is part of the problem. Adolescence is the time of growth and change for young people. They are confused by their parents' use of drugs, including alcohol. They are apt to turn to a group of their peers to discover what it is all about. They want to experiment like their friends. In addition, they like the pleasure they get from the use of drugs. The consequences of drug use for many young people are devastating. We know if young people take drugs and alcohol, it will make them capable of anything. They will lie, cheat, steal, rob, rape, and kill. They will go out on the weekend smoke a little pot, take a few pills, and drink a little alcohol, because everyone else is doing it. They find themselves in trouble the next day because they did something wrong while under the influence. However, being under the influence is not an excuse. When they end up in prison, they are subject to far greater crimes than those that got them there. Other inmates may rape or kill them. At the least, other inmates will physically and mentally abuse them. Their parents cannot help them. They are on their own. Prison is not a nice place to be. You have to join the crowd to survive. What can we do? This book emphasizes parents teaching their children the evil of drugs by word and deed. Will it keep them on the straight and narrow? Not necessarily but there is a much better chance that they will survive and have a good life.

Step 8. Need For Maintenance

How do I maintain my new life? If you are in recovery and have a slip, it is not a relapse. Relapse would be going back to drinking as you had been before your slip. A slip would depend on what you do tomorrow. If you are still in the your program, then the you are still in recovery. There are few who quit drinking and never take another drink or have a slip. Recovery is a lifelong process. I am reminded of what Mark Twain said concerning smoking: "It's easy to quit smoking; I have quit a hundred times." This is true of addicts. They have all quit many times. Staying "quit" is the problem for most. Eventually most realize that their success is only possible by keeping their heads on straight. They need to follow a maintenance program. Relapse is a process. You are always in danger of thinking like you used to and finding yourself back where you came from. What are some of the warning signs? Thinking, *It will not hurt to have of little secret sip or slip. I have been doing very well, no one will know. I do not need to go to my support group all the time. A little lie now and then does not really matter. Just one little drink. I think I am a social drinker anyway.* When you start to think like this, you are on a slippery slope and had better watch out.

A lot of study has gone into the subject of relapse. Today, relapse is seen as part of recovery. However, some on the parole board insist that a slip is relapse. Statistics show that approximately two thirds of all relapses occur within the first ninety days of quitting. This is true whether the addiction be drugs, smoking, or gambling. Studies also show that in ninety percent of cases, a single slip is followed by a full-blown relapse. Relapse does not start with the first drink. It is a process. There are warning signs like difficulty coping, interpersonal conflict, social pressure, and negative feelings.

If you remove the warning signs, you stop the cycle of addiction. The last thing is taking the drink. What you do the next day is important. Don't forget, your addiction will be there as long as you live.

Chapter 10
VIOLENCE AND ANGER

Years ago there was a radio program marked by the slogan, "Who knows what evil lurks in the hearts of men? The Shadow knows." There is something evil about violence. Even good men become violent. It is not unknown for correctional and peace officers to be violent. Domestic violence is a terrible crime and is on the increase. Approximately one out of ten women are abused. A nationwide survey in the United States found that about one of eight husbands had assaulted their wives in that year. It occurs in families from all occupations. All racial, socio-economic, religious, and educational backgrounds are represented in statistics. Professional men, unskilled laborers, and the unemployed are involved in violence.

Violence is often the result of anger that is out of control. Anger is an emotion that we all experience under some circumstances. Some people have very short fuses, get angry quickly, and often express their anger in violent acts. Violence at its worst involves killing and at its least attacking another, often in order to control or to get even. Violence can be physical, emotional, sexual, or any combination. Directed toward children, physical violence would include sexual assault, beating, starving, scaring physically, putting in a dark closet, pushing, hitting, burning, threatening, degrading, choking, use of weapons, murder. Any of these can be lethal. Psychological violence directed toward children would involve the withdrawal of love and acceptance. In addition, all attempts to destroy their self-esteem, treating them like an adult, not letting them be themselves, witnessing violence between parents, embarrassing them before friends, isolating them from friends, large expectations, blaming, and comparisons. This emotional abuse cuts deeper than the physical. Sexual abuse includes the following: unwanted touching, fondling, looks, sexual comments, incest rape, sexual murder, pornography, watching parents have sex.

Violence is a very big problem in our world today. It is growing at an alarming rate due in part to the increase in gangs and drugs. Drugs lower the inhibitions of people and increase the possibility of them acting in a harmful manner. It was thought years ago that by society doing away with seemingly violent acts like corporal and capital punishment, it would decrease the violence in the community. This unfortunately has not been the case. Violence is on the increase. Fifty years ago, our streets were relatively safe. You could go for a walk after dark. In many homes, doors were left unlocked. Home invasion was unknown. Not only has the number of violent acts increase dramatically, but also the severity of those acts has increased. Today guns are frequently used in crimes.

Everyone is capable of committing a violent act under certain circumstances. There is such a thing as acceptable violence. If one has mentally processed the violent action as necessary as in war or home invasion, violence may be in order. However, these are violent reactions that need to be immediate. Fortunately, most are not called upon to take such action. Our concern in this book is with spousal violence and violence toward children.

Many people call hockey and boxing violent sports because people are attacking others. There is another dimension to these attacks when one becomes angry and loses it. At that point, it moves from acceptable to unacceptable violence. Anger leads to the desire to injure or destroy the other person. Anger and violence do not go together. Anger always needs to be dealt with by a thinking person not a reacting person. Putting anger and violence together is likely to end in a crime of passion. Anger is a relative emotion. You can be mildly upset, or you can be seeing red. Your reaction depends on your maturity and the situation you are facing.

Violence is wrong. The Bible clearly forbids it. It says, "No one shall make them afraid."

Jesus says to his followers, "It will be very bad for a person if he makes one of these weak persons sin. It would be better for him to have a millstone tied around his neck and be drowned in the sea."

Violence is wrong because every person regardless of age, race, sex or social status has value and needs to be treated with respect. They are created in God's image. They are not to be beaten up. Do not view them as junk. If you fantasize about a person's bad point, you treat them as less than human. Do not belittle them so you can abuse them. If you cannot stop thinking bad about another person, get out of the situation. Something is wrong with your thinking. It is not realistic. You need to get your head on straight. The best way to do that is to talk over how you are thinking with someone else.

There are many adverse affects of violence. Think of the effect on the children. They are the real losers. They are learning that violence controls. Men can control stupid women. Children see mother as setting them up. Therefore, they are angry with both mother and father. These children usually learn not to trust. They usually blame themselves for the situation. They learn that anger equals violence. The reactions are extreme in these homes. It is all right to hit people you love. The children are taught to be ashamed of themselves and their families. Hitting does the parent more good than the child because it reduces the parent's stress. It shows the child how the chain works. Daddy is boss and is on Mom.

Mom is on the child. The child is on the dog. The child ends up with a thin skin. The control is on the outside, not the inside. Many of these children get into negative behavior just to try to cope. How does this child survive? He probably acts out, withdraws, is an uptight overachiever, or he may do the opposite and becomes an underachiever. Many skip school because of problems at home. Many suffer from nightmares, blaming, aggression, and chemical abuse to black out what is going on. The effect is destructive. Unless there is an intervention, it is bad news for their future.

Child abuse and neglect are very serious crimes. They can result in serious damage to the physical and emotional development of a child. These children often have a poor self-concept, a higher level of aggression, anxiety, and a lower level of impulse control and self-destructiveness. As a consequence as they grow older, they may display more antisocial behavior and the chances of success in life are hindered. Child sexual abuse may have serious and permanent affects on children. These effects include becoming an abuser themselves, prostitution, a problem of trusting males, and a negative self-image. If you have a problem of offending in this area, you need the help of a good professional counselor. See one for the sake of the child, if not for your own sake.

What is the real cause of domestic violence? Men give many reasons for battering women, but

men must take responsibility. I am responsible.
I can't blame others. I get angry, but I am
responsible for how I deal with my anger. Anger
is a human emotion. We all get angry, but we do
not all lash out. Stress, poor communication, and
alcohol all contribute to the problem, but are not
the reason for violence. The reason for violence
is power and control. Traditionally, when a man
goes into a relationship, he thinks he is king. He
thinks it's a hierarchy. He is king, his wife is queen,
and the children are the servants. His house has
thick walls to keep others out. At work he may not
be the boss or the head, but home is his castle.
A woman may be very difficult to get along with,
but often hasn't much of a choice if she leaves
the situation. A man can usually get out of a
relationship easier than a woman.

In a recent counseling session, a man said,
"I think the husband and wife should be partners."
I said, '"You mean, like 50/50 partnership, like
equals?'' He said, "Well, not quite, maybe like
51/49 partnership." That was his problem. He
can't understand why he is having a problem in
the relationship. You just have to look at our male
heroes. Who are they? Brad Pit, Tom Cruise, Clint
Eastwood, Chris Brown, Sean Penn. Who are our
female heroes? Rihanna, Madonna, Britney Spears,
Jennifer Lopez. Look at the characteristics of these
males. They are, big, strong, powerful, independent,
rich, and in control. What about the characteristics
of our women heroes? They are, sexy, great bodies,

weak, and caretakers. What is the implication of this? It is that men are in control. Men are good. Women are bad. If they don't do what they are told, they deserve to be disciplined. It is easy to see where the root of the problem of violence is.

Many men don't handle feelings very well. They have learned that to have feelings is not manly. They have learned to deny their feelings, to be a tough. They need to learn to feel and share their feelings. Some become violent when they become angry.

Example 5

CYCLE OF VIOLENCE

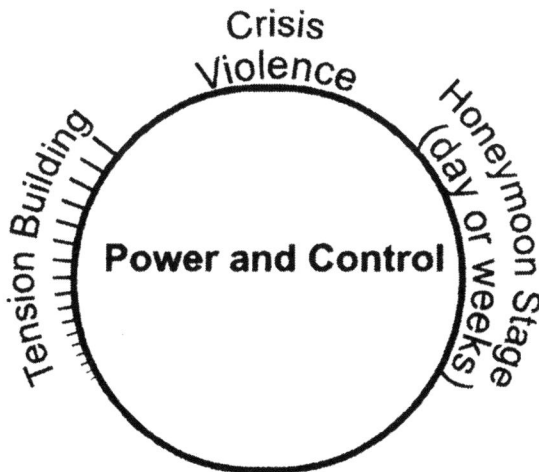

In domestic violence, there is a cycle. There is a pattern to the violence. We begin on the honeymoon. Things are all right in the home.

Husband and wife are getting along better than ever, then something happens and the tension begins to build again. Things like worry, frustration, confusion, hurt, sadness, or loneliness are put in the top of the funnel.

Example 3

FUNNEL

Worried Frustrated Confused Hurt Sad Lonely

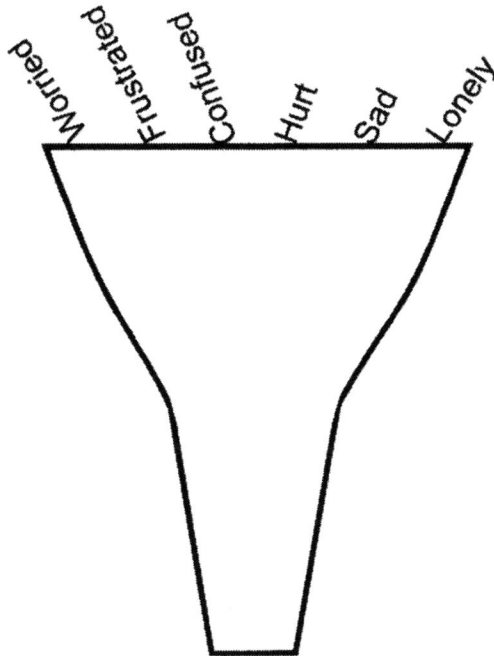

As they run down the funnel, they are all pushed together. It is just too much. The anger experienced is too much. There is an explosion that results in violence. The cycle usually speeds up and gets more violent as time goes on.

Chapter 11
HOW TO HANDLE ANGER

If you are an abuser or a victim of abuse, you need to see a family counselor or get into a group that deals with family violence. However, in case you are not willing or able to do either of these things, here are some ideas that can help you deal with your problem. These are things to help you get off the merry-go-round. You need to change your thinking. Your problem is your thinking. This must change. You must change from being a reacting person to a thinking person.

Example 4

HOW MEN SEE VIOLENCE

Men see violence like this

How you think about things is important. My wife is late coming home. I wonder where she is. What is she doing? Maybe she's met Jim,

who she went around with before she met me.
I begin my negative self-talk without knowing
what happened. Actually, she had missed her
bus, but I have to think the worst. I have to make
a mountain out of a molehill. How you interpret a
situation is important. If I add my negative self-talk
to other stuff going down, then watch ou

What part does stress play in violence? Stress
is not the cause of violence. We are all stressed
at times, but we are not all violent. Stress builds
up until some people blow. They are just like a
balloon. You keep blowing the balloon until it
breaks. What can be done to lower the stress? The
biggest thing is to get out of the situation. Make
use of a support person. We all need a support
person to whom we can talk and ventilate our
hostilities. Their feedback will help us see things
more realistically.

You need to be aware of how stress builds
up. It just doesn't happen that one blows up
and is violent. There are physical clues like being
lightheaded, tightening in the shoulders and
neck, being unable to sleep, tightening in the
stomach. There are thoughts of hitting someone
to show them who is boss and in control. There
are emotional clues as well. Under every violent
situation, there is hurt or fear. Are you hurting or
fearful when you become violent? You need to
become more aware of your stress level. When
you are being stressed, take a timeout. Find a way

to relax. It may be walking, running, listening to music, or something else.

It is important to get in touch with your feelings. Most people are surprised when they see a list of feelings we all experience. How many feelings do you experience? Your list would probably include anger, fear, sadness, worry, joy, happiness, and a few more. It would probably include only ten feelings at the most. However, a decent list would include 160 feelings. It is important for you to realize that you have all kinds of feelings. You may say, "I'm feeling anger." Are you sure? Maybe you are feeling afraid and frustrated.

People react to the same situation in different ways. This guy goes to see the doctor. The doctor's door is locked. He pounds on the door and then sits down. He's up again in two minutes pounding on the door. He is getting mad. This other guy finds the doctor's door locked. He chooses to sit down and wait quietly, enjoying the beautiful day. You have here two very different reactions to the same situation. Why not choose to change your reaction to a situation instead of getting all upset? Relax and do something else to reduce the tension. Try talking to someone. Try thinking positive thoughts instead of negative thoughts and see the difference it makes.

3. Breaking the tension by laughing at your situation will help. You know it takes two to tango.

Both you and your wife need to see that you are setting each other up. You're playing a game. However, it's a dangerous game. Someone said, "There are no victims, only volunteers." Women don't like being beaten up, but they sure like the honeymoon after. Some people do things to irritate the other. They add fuel to the fire. It always takes two to correct the situation in a home. If you can see the game that is going on and laugh at it, the tension is lessened. Otherwise, the game continues until the explosion. Violent people are over-reacting. They take situations too seriously. They are responding inappropriately. A little thing becomes a big thing. Next time you are having an argument with your spouse stop for a moment and ask, "What are we arguing about?" Often you will find it is next to nothing. It seems you just want to have an argument. Your response to a little argument is exaggerated.

There are different styles of communication. There is a control style. This is represented by blaming, the word "you," accusing, or silence. There is also a "we" style. This two-way style explores the relationship. You make the choice as to the style. You can jump into either style. The knowledge about violence in this chapter will help reduce the anxiety that surrounds it.

What about jealousy? Everyone experiences jealousy, just like everyone experiences worry. Jealousy is like a rocking chair. No matter how much time you spend being jealous, it doesn't get you anywhere. It can eat at you and hurt you as well as the person targeted by your jealousy. On the other hand, for some it can cause a response of love and caring. The majority of married people consider that there is something magical and mystical between them. Their relationship is very special. When tampered with, there is apt to be jealousy. A hug or kiss from someone other than their spouse could be a problem for some but not for others. Going for dinner, spending too much time with someone other than your spouse could cause problems.

A serious problem might be violence or threats of violence. Coupled with alcohol, jealousy can cause serious violence. There are some things that can help people who are having difficult because of jealousy. Jealousy is an indication that things are not the best in the relationship. It is likely there is a communication problem. Seeing a counselor or getting involved in a marriage enrichment course could help. In fact, some information about jealousy and communication might be all that is needed. Assertiveness training could be a big help where there is a problem of jealousy. In many cases, communication and assertiveness training will solve the problem. If they don't, you need to see a counselor.

What about alcohol and violence? There is a relationship between alcohol and family violence.

Alcohol contributes to family violence in some cases. Some people's personalities changed radically when they drink. Sober, they are the nicest people you could meet. Drunk, they are hostile even to the point of being violent. Others are more violent in the home when they quit their drinking. When they drank, they would leave home and explode on the street. Now they stay home sober and explode there. There are also those who don't drink who are extremely violent in their homes.

Most people who are violent have experienced violence in their homes when children. Abusive homes produce abusive people. Someone said, "I fight when I drink because that is what I saw in my home. My parents and brothers and sisters fought physically all the time." So physical violence is considered okay in some homes. It is an acceptable expression of one's anger.

We may conclude that alcohol doesn't cause violence. Violence is a learned behavior. However, alcohol does contribute to the violence in that it lowers natural inhibitions and allows some people to vent their anger in violent ways. It also helps some people release their repressed anger in destructive ways. Alcohol is frequently involved in violence. Someone said, "Every alcoholic has hit his wife at least once." Where there is both alcoholism and violence, you must deal with both. You can't deal with the violent behavior without dealing with the alcoholism. You can't get a person's head on straight while they are chemically dependent. The alcoholic is extremely self-centered and can't see things from another point of view. On the other hand, to treat the alcoholic and not the violence, we can still have a very violent person. The violence may change in kind. Inhibitions stop the person from actually hitting, but the mental abuse of the spouse may increase. Both the alcohol and the violence need to be addressed.

The family you lived in when you were a young child has a great influence on the rest of your life. Your experiences before you were six years old are most important. The way in which your parents related to each other is a model of how you relate to your spouse. The way in which your parents related to you will have great influence on how you relate to your children. You have probably heard, "If you want to know what your wife will be like, look at her mother." To be the best parent possible you need to take a parenting course. You need to consider what is best for your child. Remember that what you do, your children will probably do when they have children. If there is violence of any kind, physical, emotional, or sexual, in the home, it is apt to be copied by others in the home.

Assertiveness training can be a big help. Being assertive means being open and honest about what you think and allowing the other person to be the same. It means agreeing to disagree without being disagreeable. It is okay for you to express what you think, and the other person has the same right also. Opinions need to be expressed in your normal manner of talking.

If you are not assertive, others will violate your rights. They will run the show, and you will end up carrying some anger within.

Non-assertiveness avoids conflict at the moment but results in lower self-esteem and the growth of resentment that weakens the relationship. In other words, you feel like a wimp.

If you are aggressive, you are disregarding the other person's rights. You are trying to beat up on the other person. It might involve raising your voice or yelling. It is likely to involve getting even with the other person in somewhat sneaky ways. It is not healthy.

Being assertive does not mean that you will get your way or persuade the other person that you are right, but it will make you feel that you at least got to express how you think and feel. The other person knows what you think and what you need. On a line, put the numbers 1 to10—1 is aggression, 10 is non-aggression. Assertiveness comes in the middle of the line. Where do you fit? You are seeking understanding, not agreement.

Chapter 12
HOW TO DO AN INTERVENTION

A person has ended up on the road of life with a serious addiction. It is a road that leads to destruction. Soon the cuffs will be put on them. They just can't stop travelling on the road they are on, even though it is not getting them anywhere. They can find all kinds of excuses for continuing their present behavior. When they do manage to stop their addiction for a bit, a problem or challenge comes along. They slip back into their addictive behavior. Most of their old friends and family cannot stand to have them around any more because their behavior is not appropriate. They say things that are impolite. They frequently get angry and at times are physically violent. They have lost their self-esteem. Their life has become centered on their addiction. That is what they live for. What is going to stop the merry-go-round? Something needs to happen to break the cycle of their craziness. If something doesn't happen quickly, they are in real trouble. There needs to be an intervention.

Group interventions have proven to be effective. Here, a number of friends of an addict gather together with the addicted person and confront him/her with their inappropriate behavior. Other types of intervention would include the intervention by an individual. This could be a doctor, counsellor, or friend. They would seek to help the person look realistically at the harmful effects of their addiction. They encourage them to get the help they require. There are some addicts where the intervention is an act of God. Something traumatic happens to them. It could be a serious illness or a situation where they almost kill a person or get killed themselves. The shock helps them come to their senses, and they make a decision to do something about their problem.

One evening a family of friends gather in a living room for coffee. Their friend, who is an addict, has been invited. The group tries to be friendly and kind. The person in charge announces, primarily to the addict, the purpose of the gathering. They are going to individually share with him what he means to each one and how his addiction has affected them. This gathering is emotionally charged for everyone. Tears will be shed. It is the hope that this kind of gathering will get the addict to see the affect of his behavior on his friends and give him a desire to do something about his addiction. He is confronted with the affect of his addiction on each one, along with words of encouragement to seek help for his problem.

When an individual does an intervention, friendship is very important. The steps referred to in Building a Relationship (Chapter 15) and in

Mentoring (Chapter 16) should be taken by the friend before an intervention is attempted. If the person doing the intervention has been able to communicate that they really care for the other person, the addict may raise the problem of their addiction themselves. This is best, as they are asking for help and encouragement. Such an intervention is more likely to meet with positive results. If the counsellor has the gift of speaking from the heart, it will be a big help. The best picture of an individual intervention is that of a counsellor speaking from the heart to a friend.

An intervention must be done with love—that is, tough love. The loving thing to do is tell the addict the truth. They need to face their situation realistically. Minimizing their addiction is not going to help. In fact, it might be enabling them to continue their addiction. Their situation is very serious, often a matter of life and death. Because you love them, because you care, you're going to tell them the truth, even if the truth hurts. This is showing them real love even though at the time they will probably think otherwise. Remember, because of their addiction, their thinking is messed up. The other side is that our love must be unconditional. It doesn't give up. We go on loving no matter what the response.

It is normal for people to minimize their problem. They do not want to do something to change. But their problem is depressing as it cries for them to do something about it. To deal with it or to admit it is upsetting. By minimizing it, they may continue to live with their addiction even though it is destroying them and others. They have lots of excuses. "I have no time to attend classes that might help me. I don't have any money to pay for the treatment, and besides that I don't want to be associated with other addicts. My friends will think I am some kind of nut. I can handle things on my own and don't want to admit my problem."

We question whether we should intervene or not. Is this the right time to approach this person ? We wonder what the consequences may be. Maybe they will be upset and walk out. The result could be positive or negative. There is the temptation to do nothing and not risk a negative response. We may decide to put it off because it's too upsetting. It's likely to get emotional, and many of us don't like upsetting, unpredictable situations, which could go either way. We might drive this person to hang or shoot himself or herself. There are no guarantees that confronting our friend will have a positive result.

The sparks are likely to fly in an intervention because a person with little or no self-esteem is being confronted. In a group intervention, the addict will feel that his old friends are all against him. He is terribly outnumbered. The addict is being asked to change, to leave something that has become very precious to him/her—their addiction, their comforting friend, actually their life itself. They are being asked to change now and live without their addiction, which seems impossible. In fact, they've already tried to stop, and it has not worked. Interventions are asking a lot of the addict, to give up what he/she is living for. In spite of everyone becoming emotionally upset, such interventions can work if the time is right. Many different interventions may contribute to change in a person's life.

People need to be confronted with the simple truth that their addiction is destroying them as well as many others. The others include the children of our world, who very much need examples of responsible behavior by parents and adults. We need to do a much better job than we have been doing as role models.

When people face their addiction, they need lots of encouragement. This is where the 12-step groups have been a tremendous help. The addict has been comforted by his addiction. He is lonely and lost without it. The pain of quitting can very easily draw him/her back into the addiction. It is not uncommon to stop many times before a person meets with success. Addictions are for life, so one can easily slip back into them. There is also the real possibility of replacing one addiction with another.

We sometimes reject people who have problems. We get angry with them because of their problem. We don't know how to deal with them because of their problem. We need to work on understanding and accepting those who are different. They need to know that we care. Regardless of where they are presently on their journey, they are humans and therefore have value and need to be treated with respect, dignity, and an example of what is good and proper, not labeled as worthless.

Chapter 13
TAKING RESPONSIBILITY FOR YOUR CHOICES

If there is to be forward movement in people's lives, they need to accept the fact that they make things happen or that their choices have consequences. To believe that things "just happen" is wrong. To believe that others cause things to happen will stop a person dead in their tracks. Our problem is that we tend to stay where we are. We are creatures of habit and don't easily change our thinking or acting. Some even think that being stuck in a rut is a good thing. The problem is, that doesn't get them anywhere. Many of us need to get out of the rut we are travelling in and get on a better road. For the person who has been in prison, the sad fact is prison has conditioned them not to take responsibility. They are used to being taken care of and not making choices for themselves. This is not good training for living on the street.

Some have been born with eight cylinders, others with six, and still others with only two—and they are none too good. However, when it comes to what you make of your life, it has more to do with the choices you make than with what you have been given. This chapter is about taking responsibility for your choices.

Some go through life blaming others for their rotten luck. They prefer to sit in their rocking chair talking about why they are losers. It's always someone else's fault. "I am where I am in my life because of my mother or my father." "It's the teacher's fault." "It's the systems fault." "It's the fault of the police," and on and on it goes. They don't see that they have made choices in life and those choices have consequences. If you choose to mess around with certain people, you will become like them. If you choose to lie in bed most of the day instead of getting up and working, the consequence is you have no money.

The reason blame is a waste of time is that it always looks back on something you cannot change. Whatever the past be, good or bad, it is over. To spend time and energy on the past isn't going to change it one bit. It is over, done with. Let it be. Focus on what is ahead. Looking back focuses on death. Looking ahead focuses on life. Taking responsibility always looks to the future. Successful people don't worry and complain about the past. Taking responsibility for your choices is the way to a happy, successful life.

Today, you have a self-image. It could be positive or negative. If positive, you have a good self-image. If negative, you have a poor self-image. It is likely that your self-image is up and down. There is a big difference between

98

people when it comes to their self-image and their choices because there is a close relationship between our self-image and our choices. Those who say, "I can't do it," represent a poor self-image. People with a positive self-image say, "Yes, I can," and get on with the job. If your self-image is poor, you must change it if you are to succeed in life. Remember that your choices are tied to your self-esteem. If your self-esteem is poor, you're not going to get anywhere. Here are some steps to take to help with your self-esteem and with the choices you make in life. The following steps will require some discipline.

First, watch your mental diet. Feed your mind on materials such as found in Chapter 3 on self-esteem. Find some books and meditative material that will help you think positively. You can do it.

Second, as much as you can, associate with positive people, These people are the winners. Remember, you become like the people with whom you associate.

Finally, watch your health. If you feel good physically, you will find it easier to be positive. Be sure to get enough sleep. Eat the proper food. Get plenty of exercise so that you're healthy and feel good. These three things—what you feed your mind, the people you hang out with, and staying healthy—will encourage a positive attitude in you.

Why is it necessary for you to accept responsibility for your life? Making the decision to take responsibility, which means realizing, "If it's to be, it's up to me," is going to be hard. It took many years for you to get where you are now and to change roads is going to be difficult. But it can be done. Others have done it. You can too. To change, you need to change your thinking. If you are going to change your life and get somewhere, it's your thinking that needs some work done on it. Make a commitment to change your thinking now and get started today. You must be dedicated to taking responsibility for your choices. This means dedicating your life to taking responsibility for your choices. You need to focus on doing this. Make this your top priority in life. People often respond to the question of where they are going by saying, "I'm just going." They don't know where they are going. The payoff for taking responsibility for your choices in life is the healthiest, happiest, and most successful life possible.

Rather than suggest seven steps to successful living in this chapter, here is just one step that can change your life. The essential step to change your life is to make a plan. You've got to have a plan if you're going to get somewhere. Otherwise you will just go around in circles the rest of your life. Start today by making a plan. Where do you want to go? Take some time deciding this. It's a very important decision. You need a long-term plan that includes a goal you want to reach in the next few months. You also need a short-term plan including a goal for tomorrow. This is a plan for just one day and should be made tonight for tomorrow.

This must be done every night of your life. The purpose of having a plan for each day is to continually boost your self-image. This will help you keep going. Take the goal for the day and think of the steps you need to take to reach it. Then tonight you can be happy that you accomplished what you set out to do today. If you are having a problem motivating yourself to reach a goal or take a step, try a simple thing like rewarding yourself when you reach the goal. Instead of having your cup of coffee now, save the coffee as a reward when you finish the job at hand. Your short-term goal is a small piece of your long-term goal. Your goal should be reasonable but not easy. Your goal needs to be something that challenges you. Then you will feel good when you reach it and you will be growing. Remember, if you look forward, not backward, your life will always have meaning and purpose.

Life is a process, and it is the process that is fun. Success is not arriving. Success is the process of moving toward your goal. By the time you reach one goal in your life, you will have set your sights on another goal. It's the journey that's important. That's the fun of living. If you ever arrive, you are dead.

Successful people don't go through life hoping to win the lottery. If you are sitting there waiting for something good to happen to you, forget it because it won't. Get busy by following the blueprint set out in this chapter. Set your long-term goal and your daily goal, and then get busy. And you know what? Something great will happen along the way. Successful people know that the harder they work to reach their goals the luckier they become.

Every day of your life you are given the same number of hours as everyone else. What are you going to do with those hours—use them or lose them? If you don't use those hours, you're going to lose them. If you're not using your hours, you're going backwards. You are on the road to self-destruction. Use them, and you're on the road to happiness, success, and the best life possible.

Chapter 14
FINDING A JOB

Studies show that criminals who get a job when released are less likely to return to a life of crime. The bad news is that for many criminals, getting a job is difficult. The good news is it is possible for criminals to get a job. The two reasons for the difficulty are the criminal and the employer. In the case of the criminal the problem is: poor education, little or no employment history, lack of motivation. Frequently, the offender is unemployed when arrested. A sizable number cannot read. Educational and job programs that would help the criminal find employment after release are not always available while incarcerated because of cost. Programs to help criminals upon release vary from place to place and from time to time. The cost of such programs severely limits the services offered. Where available, job programs offer services such as counseling, help with an Internet search, resume writing, job leads, and preparation for an interview. Programs also help by providing clients with forms, fax machines, computers, and newspapers.

Criminals' problems are complicated and include inappropriate public relationship skills, lack of job and living skills, chemical abuse, learning disabilities, and mental illness. Criminals in the job market compete with others who have fewer problems, which makes it difficult. The prospective employer is concerned with the possibility of violence on the job. In addition, the lack of education can be problem. Work has to be done with employers to dispel their fears of hiring an criminal. To dispel the myth, criminals can help by proving themselves and doing a great job for their employer.

To be successful, criminals need to improve their self-image. Just getting a job like most other people their age is a boost. It makes them feel they are as good as others. They are worthwhile. It keeps them busy and gives structure to their lives that will help them keep out of trouble. Instead of being down on themselves, they are much happier, and so are their families. Jobs of any type are good for one's mental health. If you can't get a job that pays you money right away, you should spend some time volunteering. Besides giving your life some structure, it will help you feel better about your existence. You are contributing something to the community. Volunteering can also help with your resume. Some people have found jobs through volunteering. When you don't have a job, your job is finding a job. This will help you from getting discouraged and becoming a couch potato. Get up in the morning as if you had a paying job, go to the job center, see what help they can give you that day and get busy.

JOB SEARCH TIPS

Here are some job search tips that have helped others. What would you like to do? Now don't be too fussy. The main thing at this point is to get a job. Any job is better than not getting your dream job. Ask yourself, "What can I do? What can I offer an employer?" You need to build a job history so you can get reference letters to get that job you really want later. What can you see yourself doing in order to get a job?

LEADS FOR A JOB SEARCH

1. What about your friends? Everyone is a source since many jobs are never posted. There is truth in the old saying: "It's not what you know but who you know that matters." Countless people have found jobs through a friend's recommendation.
2. Most communities have job centers offering a number of services that can be helpful in finding a job. A job center has some real advantages for you. It will help keep you motivated in your job search by giving advice and by supplying you with helpful leads.

3. The computer is also a real help in doing a job search. Job centers will supply the computer and show you how to use it for a job search.
4. Newspapers have traditionally been a source of employment ads for many.
5. One other thing you might try is cold calling. It has worked for many. Say you would like to learn to be a bricklayer's helper—the guy who mixes the mortar. Find a bricklayer, tell him of your dream, and ask him if he has any ideas that might help you. Be sure to make use of every lead in your job search.

POINTERS FOR YOUR JOB INTERVIEW

1. Be sure to arrive five minutes early. To arrive five minutes late does not show respect and could easily mean you don't get the job.
2. Show your resume to as many as possible. Keep it to one page.
3. Get as much information on the job you're applying for as possible.
4. Be polite; manners impress.
5. Once you are in the hot seat, sit straight, smile, and try to relax.
6. Tell them you're a hard worker.
7. Be clean, tidy.
8. Getting a job is most important, not the pay. The pay will come if you work hard.

When you get the job, be at work five minutes early every day. Be willing to stay a little late if your boss needs a hand. The brownie points you earn will pay off later. Yes, you may have to bite your tongue at times, but remember you're not the boss.

Chapter 15
HOW TO HELP CRIMINALS AND THEIR FAMILIES

Even though other chapters touch on relationships, this chapter is included because of the importance of relationships with criminals, and their families.

How you see criminals and their families, whether good or bad, determines how you will treat them. Try to see criminals as humans, ordinary people like you and me—people with hopes and dreams, people who have feelings just like us. At times they're happy and at other times sad. Sometimes, they feel secure and at others scared. They get angry. They love others just as much as you do. Their feelings are similar and they are good, but like all of us not perfect. Really, they are no different than we are. If this is the way you see them, then you will give them some time and treat them just like you treat your own family and friends. We should pray for them and try to help them have their needs met. Certainly, we treat them with dignity and respect. If you do so, too, your attitude will be nonjudgmental.

On the other hand, if you see criminals as people who have been in prison and have the devil residing in them and are presently planning their next evil deed, if you see them as people who are liars and can't be trusted, or are just waiting to manipulate you, if you see them as losers, then you will feel that they should be locked up for life and the key thrown away. You will believe they need longer sentences and less humane treatment. Your attitude will be judgmental.

Criminals hunger for a good friend. This is where you are needed. William Glasser in his book *Reality Therapy* said, "We at all times in our lives must have at least one person who cares about us and about whom we care for ourselves. If we do not have this essential person, we will not be able to fulfill our basic needs. If a prisoner or castaway loses the conviction that this essential human [cares] about what is happening to him, he will lose touch with reality, his needs will be more and more unfulfilled, or he may die or become insane."

You are needed in helping criminals and their families. They need you to become closely related to them. It will help them. Don't expect big miracles. There will be small steps—a little growth here and there. Expectancies need to be watched. If I am an criminal, I need to remind myself that I have feet of clay. It is human to fail, to go back to one's old ways. I need to learn to forgive myself when I slip. If I am trying to help an criminal, I need to realize that the person I am working with may stay out of jail longer this time than last. He may have learned a valuable lesson. There is likely some growth. At least one has learned what doesn't work. This is success.

Life for all of us is a journey in growing. The stigma of prison must be removed. These are human beings, our brothers, and sisters in the family of man. We must be available to them. We must show them our concern. Sacrifice on our part is necessary if we are to improve the situation. We need to be dedicated and willing to pay the cost of change. You can have a part in creating a better world. Jobs are needed. There is much to be done. Don't write people off. They may surprise you. There's something mystical about self-determination. Believe me, people do change. Joy awaits you as you extend a helping hand to a criminal and his/her family.

It is a sad time for the prisoners' wife and children. They are forgotten. How do they make out when Dad is in prison? It's harder, much harder on the wife and the kids. Listen to the pain in these words from a criminal's wife.

So you care about someone who is incarcerated? Me, too! How do you deal with these emotions: anger, hurt, frustration, loneliness? I am hurt because he left me alone out here. He knows what his life will be like for the next few years; mine is uncertain and some days are just chaos.

I am frustrated because it's hard to deal with this alone. When I want him to help with everyday decisions, he's not there! Then there is the neighbors, family (his and mine) and the kids! What do I do next?

And there is the system to deal with. I can't see him or talk to him about any of these feelings at my convenience. It's always on their time and terms. I forget some of the things I need to share and talk about. There is always a stranger standing there, or a glass wall, or a phone. I get tired of long lines and impersonal faces who see me as a number, not as a loving caring individual in my own right. I just want to say, "Don't judge me for this person's crime."

I work, I struggle, and sometimes I cry because things are not quite right at home. Someone is missing. I love this person and would like to make the best of a bad situation. Please save me from well-meaning friends and family who feel sorry or criticize me for staying close to this person. Sometimes they even agree with the mean things I say out of anger and frustration. I do not need someone to agree, I just want to share these feelings with someone who understands—someone just like me who has someone on the inside.

Criminals' families need help. People don't live in isolation. Working with families is a neglected area in the criminal justice system. The criminal's family may be his biological family or it could be his male friends. Family are those who you feel you belong to, those who support you. Family support during incarceration and following is critical to a successful adjustment following release. Studies have shown that men who have family support have a much better chance of not returning to a life of crime. We may not see the family healed completely but maybe it can walk again even with a limp. Just think of the losses that prisoners' families suffer: income, holidays, family get-togethers, self-image, reputation, loss of trust, friends, role model, parental rights, control, loss of dignity, intimate physical contact, freedom, privacy, support at the time of the death of a loved one. Your encouragement is needed. Children and teenagers are being neglected. We need programs for children of criminals.

Relating to an criminal is difficult. Criminals have a problem trusting others. Their lives have been taken over by others because of their poor choices. From the time of their arrest, they have lost their freedom to make choices. The prosecuting attorney speaks against them and a defense lawyer speaks for them. The criminal watches the show with little or no personal involvement. Can you feel what a criminal feels because of their situation? They may put on a good front to cover their real feelings. They need to appear strong and tough to survive in the prison world where the weak are targeted. If you trust anyone, you may not live to regret it.

The offender is imprisoned by his poor self-image, his fears, his grief, his anger, among other things like chemical abuse and addictive behavior. So building a relationship with the offender is not easy. There is the issue of confidentiality. If an offender lets down his guard and lets you become a friend, you need to realize that what he shares is between you and him/her. He/she does not share this with many. It is a difficult step for the offender to be transparent, so you must value the relationship.

Many criminals are depressed and feel guilty. Dr. Berne wrote a book years ago entitled, *I'm Okay, You're Okay.* In it he presented four ways that people relate: "I'm okay, you're okay," healthy position; "I'm okay, you're not okay," superior position; "I am not okay, you're okay," inferior position; "I'm not okay, you're not okay," criminal position. In this position, it doesn't matter what you do. What we are faced with is trying to get a person to the healthy position, "I'm okay, you're okay." This involves building a person's self-esteem.

Many of a group of 300 criminals I worked with were born again. They have had their eyes opened to the craziness in their lives and decided to live lives that are more responsible. Many of them believe that God has forgiven them, but they still suffer from guilt and low self-esteem. They need a lot of affirmation. I say "a lot" because most prisoners have been told over and over again, "You're not okay; you are stupid, you're lazy, you will never make it, you're bad." We need to find something good about a person and praise them for it. Many criminals can only see their failure and the bad that they have done in their lives. The space they are in does not result in joyful, successful living. We are giving people burdened with guilt and low self-esteem a wonderful gift when we affirm them. We all need to feel good about ourselves. Will you help?

Chapter 16
HOW TO BE A MENTOR

This chapter is for those of you who are ready to help others. Mentoring is like teaching, counseling, and sponsoring. It is taking responsibility for the growth of another person. Some mentoring is done with a formal arrangement, but much effective mentoring is done informally. In both cases the mentor gives the person being mentored serious attention. A mentor is a role model that a person looks up to because of the way the mentor thinks and acts. This chapter is concerned with mentors who represent the finer qualities of life, such as unselfishness, honesty, goodness, self-esteem, and kindness. Some people naturally have these characteristics; others have to develop them. Your mentor is someone you would like to imitate because his or her qualities appeal to you. A person may have more than one mentor—many do.

A commitment to mentoring is very important because mentoring is serious business. Why do people want to be mentors? The main reason a person wants to be a mentor is that they want to help other people. This is a common desire of many people. Mentoring is the work of Jesus. In his day, Jesus was always busy helping hurting people. Possibly you have had a mentor in your own life—someone you have wanted to be like, someone who helped you through a tough time. It might have been a family member or a complete stranger who became one of your best friends and had a great influence on you. You want to be like them. God has placed in your heart a desire to help others by word and deed.

Friendliness is key to mentoring because of the necessity of establishing a close, positive relationship. Remember to smile and relax.

Mentoring is more than just talking. It is getting to know each other at a deep level. Something happens between people when they do this. There is a real sharing that is open and honest, and as a result of this there is caring in the relationship. The mentor is willing to sacrifice in order to help the person they are mentoring.

A mentor needs to accept the person they are mentoring even if the person has committed some terrible crime. Remember every human is worthwhile. God loves everyone just as much as he loves you. You can't help a person whom you don't accept as a human being. This does not mean that you approve of their behavior, but you need to communicate to them that you accept them just as they are with all their baggage, all the good and bad in them.

A mentor needs to be mature. Maturity is not a matter of age. Frequently the best mentor for a young person will be another young person. Maturity in a mentor will depend on one's life experiences. The mentor will have enough experience to be able to look at the situation of the person being mentored objectively. The mentor also needs sufficient maturity to keep things shared confidential, and to be a consistent role model.

MENTORING SKILLS

Here are some skills you need to develop to be a mentor.

A mentor needs to be a good listener. This is the most important thing you do for the person you are mentoring. Communication is not just talking. It is understanding each other. Through active listening, you show a person that you are listening to them by repeating back to them what you heard them say verbally and through their body language. Perhaps they are very angry about their home situation. They express this by word and the tone of their voice. You might say to them, "I see that you are angry at what has happened to you at home. I would be angry too if I were in your shoes." This will show that you are paying attention and care enough about them to do so. It bonds you to the person you are trying to help. It shows that you accept them as a worthwhile person, seen in your caring enough to really listen to what they're saying. It doesn't mean that you agree with their attitude. You may not. But you understand their attitude.

Active listening also shows that you care enough to let them have control. You let them take the lead in the conversation. You don't push them. This communicates respect and builds trust.

Finally, active listening encourages people to explore their problems. It's like holding a mirror up for people to look at their words and feelings. They end up getting a much better picture of themselves, and a clearer idea of what action they should take.

It is a healing activity for the talkers. They get some bad feelings off their chest. By sharing things that are bothering them, they often feel they have unloaded a burden. When you actively listen, you show you care.

A mentor needs to remember the names of people because people like to hear their name. If you have a problem remembering names, here are two ideas that should help. If it is a new person with a new name, try using the name frequently. After meeting with them picture them in your mind. This usually is not a problem. Then repeat their name. Do this several times over a few days, and you should not have a problem next time you meet. Another good way of remembering a person's name is through association. They may remind you of someone else you know with the same name, or they may remind you of something. Just associate the picture in your mind with them a number of times, and you should have no problem with their name next time you meet.

You need to pay attention to a person's body language if you are seeking to mentor them. If they are open, they will be relaxed, which would indicate that they are receiving what you're saying. On the other hand, if they give evidence of being uptight, evidence like fidgeting, continually moving their legs, avoiding eye contact, or crossing their legs, they are likely uncomfortable with you and your questions and are shutting you out. You need to back off in this case for you are pushing them too much. They are rejecting you and your message. By backing off and coming back to the subject later, you will likely get further with them. Often if you can show that you are on their side, that you are understanding them, they will be open about those things that really matter to them, the things that they need to process at this time in their life.

The relationship is not just for the pleasure of talking. There will also be a time to give advice and point out mistakes. In order for this to happen and be accepted, there must be trust in the relationship. Correcting is often best done by reinforcing positive behavior in the other person. Tact is necessary in the process.

There are times when asking a question may be in order. For instance a question can keep things going when they begin to lag. A question may be used to change the direction and draw attention to something you think a person should consider. Though it will probably take longer to get the answer to your question, active listening is usually the best way to go because the person is still in charge, and they don't withdraw because you're being a snoop.

How you dress shows respect, as does being polite and giving of your time and attention to another human.

Being a mentor is a high calling, so give it your best shot. A good mentor is a person who can focus on another person. Such a mentor will communicate through body language as well as words his deep interest in the person he is mentoring. He has empathy and understanding of where the person is coming from. This results in an open relationship where there is something happening between the two. The mentor is a good listener who can tactfully ask the questions that will draw the person out. The mentor has matured himself or herself through many life experiences and feels the responsibility of giving advice to another who is seeking it. He is in the position of the teacher with a student who is interested in learning. There's more to being a mentor than just being a friend and having fun together. A mentor is not a babysitter, but is someone who is seeking to help another.

Chapter 17
WHAT A RELATIONSHIP WITH GOD CAN DO FOR YOU

As we consider what a relationship with God is like, your eyes will be opened in amazement. This is an individual experience. Everyone who has such an experience describes it differently, which should not surprise us because everyone is different and everyone's experience is unique.

A relationship with God involves knowing him as a friend. It is being in touch with him, sensing or feeling his presence in your daily life. He is alive to you.

It also involves knowing God as your Savior. God is the friend of sinners. Christianity declares that Christ died for our sins on the cross. It declares that man is a sinner and that God cannot accept him because of his sin. Someone has to pay for his sins, and that is what God in Christ did on the cross. The Christian is someone who has seen his/her sins laid on Christ on the cross. The requirement for this to happen is that a person must accept Jesus Christ as her/his Savior and Lord. There is a mystery about this experience. There are millions of people on earth who have had such an experience and say that it is like being born again. Through their experience, they became alive to God. A change took place in their lives. This change resulted in a new life that is like walking with God. God is their constant companion. This experience is maintained through reading their Bible and conversing with God. It helps them face the challenges and difficulties of this life and involves the belief that God will also take care of them when they die. They will go to a better place than this world for eternity. A relationship with God involves knowing him as a friend, savior, and helper.

For a person to have such a relationship with God, there must first be openness to him. God won't break down the door to get into your life. If you choose to believe that there is no God, a relationship will not happen. However, if you're open to the idea that there may be a God and are seeking to know him, you will find him.

You will also need some knowledge about God and what the Bible says about him. It is necessary to accept God's truth as found in the Bible if you are to follow his way. The precise truth you need to accept is that God gave himself on the cross, so that if you receive him you can be forgiven and have a relationship with him.

Finally, you have to feel a need for a better life than you presently have. It could be a need for a close friend, strength, happiness, peace, or a better self-image.

What A Relationship With God Can Do For You

God makes many promises in the Bible. The best one is his promise that if you receive him, trust in him, turn to him, he will become your friend, savior, and helper. It is up to you to move toward him because he is always there waiting. He loves you and will respond. He can and will help you in every way you need help, forgiving you, walking beside you, filling you with joy and peace, and giving you a heavenly home. He is for you. He loves you with an everlasting love. He loves you now and will love you forever.

For something to happen between you and God, you must turn to God's way. A number of different words are used in the Bible to describe this turning to God. Words like believing, accepting, receiving, following, faith, and trust are used. All these words refer to turning God's way and following it. You have been traveling your own way, but you can decide to change and start to walk with God. Turning God's way is a choice you make, a free choice. Like with other choices in life, it has its consequences.

People call this a conversion experience. A conversion experience results in a new center for your life. For the Christian, that center is Jesus Christ. Instead of continuing to live one's life with self being the center, you now seek God's will for your life and start asking the question, "What would Jesus do in my situation?"

Another very important aspect of a conversion experience is that you experience the forgiveness of your sins, past, present, and future. When you accept the truth that Jesus died for your sins on the cross, you now stand before God, a-okay. You no longer are crippled by guilt. As a result, you are filled with a peace and joy you never knew before.

What is the place of the confession of sins in this process? The Bible says, "All have sinned and come short of the glory of God." Measured by the Ten Commandments, this is true of all of us. Most people are crippled by guilt, and getting rid of this guilt frees them to live life on a higher plane. Many have had an albatross of guilt hanging around their neck and through confessing their sins have found a wonderful release from their guilt. Most of us go through life with little thought of dying and meeting our Maker. Such a thought is just too depressing. However, if you are faced with a lingering death, you are likely to wonder if you are ready to meet God. You are bothered by the thought of things you have done in your life and the things you have left undone. To find peace you have to confess your sins and experience God's forgiveness. The confession gives you an experience that you are forgiven and are okay in the eyes of God. Apart from confession, there is no real peace. There are only two types of people who die well: the committed Christian and the atheist.

How is the new life maintained? Just as you need the right physical foods in order to be physically healthy, you need the right spiritual food to maintain spiritual health. Some of this food comes from daily Bible reading. You need to spend some time every day reading God's word. If you only do this occasionally, you're not going to be healthy. If you are just beginning your journey with God start by reading the Gospel of John. It's best to read slowly and listen to what God is saying to you through his word. To maintain your new life you need to also pray. Prayer is a great gift that God has given you. It can be done anywhere and at any time. God walks beside you on the journey of life. Be sure to talk with him as you walk along the road. One other thing that will help you maintain your new life is fellowship with other Christians. Followers of Christ have always gathered together. They have learned from each other and strengthened each other. When they gather, Jesus Christ is always there with them as he promised.

A Christian is not perfect. A Christian is still a human being, still has feet of clay, and still sins. The apostle Paul makes this clear in his words, "I have the desire to do what is good, but I cannot carry it out. For what I do is not the good I want to do; no, the evil I do not want to do—this I keep on doing. Now if I do what I do not want to do, it is no longer I who do it, but it is sin living in me that does it. So I find this law at work: when I want to do good, evil is right there with me. For in my inner being I delight in God's law; but I see another law at work in the members of my body, waging war against the law of my mind making me a prisoner of the law of sin at work within my members. What a wretched man I am! Who will rescue me from this body of death? Thanks be to God—through Jesus Christ our Lord! So then, I myself in my mind am a slave to God's law, but in the sinful nature a slave to the law of sin." Most Christians live better lives after their encounter with God than before. The more they have a daily diet of spiritual food, the more they will live like Jesus Christ. However, being a Christian does not mean you cannot commit some terrible crime. You can, for you are not perfect.

You will mess up because you are part of the human family. It is human to feel bad when one falls short of the bar they have set for themselves as a Christian. If you wander away from God, no longer feeding on the spiritual food of daily reading the Bible and spending time talking with God and other children of God you will begin to lose the feeling of his presence in your life. Falling into your old lifestyle will be the outcome of such behavior. Of course, God is hurt and disappointed with you. However, He does not give up on you. The good news is you can come back to God. God still loves you and will welcome you back into the relationship you had previously. Your slip does not end your relationship with God.

The prodigal son was still a son in the far country. The father was with him even when he was sinning there. We read in the Bible, "But while he was still a long way off, his father saw him and was filled with compassion for him; he ran to his son, threw his arms around him and kissed him. The son said to him, father, I have sinned against heaven and in your sight. I am no longer worthy to be called your son. But the father said to his servants, Quick! Bring the best robe and put it on him. Put a ring on his finger and sandals on his feet. Bring the fatted calf and kill it. Let's have a feast and celebrate. For this son of mine was dead and is alive again; he was lost and is found so they began to celebrate". The close relationship with his father was restored.

When you return to your daily Bible study and talking with God, the joy of your relationship with God comes back and you continue on your journey with him. To stay on target and grow in faith, the secret is daily spiritual food, Bible study, and conversing with God and fellowship with other children of God. Then whatever happens in your life or death, God is with you and will take care of you.

What is the main purpose of your life as a Christian? The main purpose of life for the Christian is to be a witness of God's love. The last words Jesus spoke to his followers while here on earth were, "Go and make disciples of all nations, baptizing them in the name of the Father and of the Son and of the Holy Spirit, and teaching them to obey everything I have commanded you. And surely I am with you always to the very end of the age". Witnessing is what gives meaning and purpose to the Christian's life. It is telling others what God has done in your life since you became a Christian. You tell them in words and in the way you live your life. You see people as God sees them. You see them as individuals with names and feelings. You see them as members of your own family. You see them as being better than you see yourself. You see them as worthy of God's love and your love.

Chapter 18
RECOMMENDATIONS

There are no quick solutions just simple solutions for preventing crime. If the following recommendations are put into practice every day in every life crime can be greatly reduced.

Education is the main key to reducing crime.
One of the best investments we can make to fight crime is to teach parenting skills and give a high level of help to our children who are at risk. Parenting programs need to be encouraged and should include programs for both young children and adolescents.

Helping adults with problems such as chemical abuse, violence, unemployment, learning disabilities, and mental illness will also help to reduce crime. The questions we need to ask are, "Why do people commit crime?" and "Did we do all we could to help them?" The key to helping adults is developing positive relationships with them and modeling the desired behavior. Relationships are a very powerful agent of change. It may be too late to help some, but not too late to help their children.

Relationships with criminals and their families are another key to reducing crime.

If you have read this book, I hope you see criminals as part of the human family. All the people of the world are family members and should be seen as such. They have names, emotions, and feelings. They are our brothers and sisters, members of our family, equally worthwhile, since we are all created in God's image. Yet, it is not a healthy family here on earth because of the brokenness that results from sin. Remember every criminal is some mother's son or daughter and needs to be prayed for and loved. There is more to everyone than meets the eye. Don't judge! There is no doubt that when we get to heaven, there will be some there we did not expect and others we expected who are not present.

We will never eliminate crime. There is in all of us self-determination. Some will choose crime no matter what. However, we can have safer streets and fewer victims of crime if we are more creative and willing to change ourselves.

Finally, the criminal's involvement is key to reducing crime.

Years ago criminals were told not to associate with known criminals. I ask you, "Whose family do criminals belong to?" Crime is a family problem. We need to have a conversation between those who we call criminals and non-criminals. Today, it's the same old adversarial system we have had forever, and it's not working. It is one-sided. We say to the criminal, "You sit down there and keep quiet, and we will decide what we're going to do with you. This guy will take care of your side, and this other guy will take care of ours. You just keep quiet. You have been bad and we don't want to hear what you have to say. You need to be put in isolation for a few years." Is this for the criminal's good or our good?

Jesus says in one of his better known conversations, "Love your neighbor as yourself." An expert fires back, "And who is my neighbor?" We don't mind following Jesus, but we want our boundaries. Carl Sandburg, the poet, once wrote when he reflected on Jesus words: "Love your neighbor as yourself. But don't take down the fence." If we could break down the wall between us, much of today's crime would be reduced. We need to have a conversation with those on the other side. Are they the missing link? We need their input in fighting crime. They belong to us. We need to help one another. Criminals are part of our family. "There go I but for the grace of God."

Announcement

Copies of this book are available at Amazon. com.

You will want to get a copy of my new companion volume containing unbelievable true stories of Angels From Hell whom I have known.

My website for anyone wishing to contact me concerning the content of this book is, criminalsfamlies.com

You may also write me at the following address. Please include a telephone number.

Byron Elsey
100 Renfrew Street
Winnipeg, MB, CANADA
R3N 1J4

3699573

Made in the USA